TRANSFORMING PERFORMANCE AT WORK

TRANSFORMING PERFORMANCE AT WORK

The Power of Positive Psychology

SARAH ALEXANDER
SERIES EDITOR: BOB THOMSON

Routledge
Taylor & Francis Group

LONDON AND NEW YORK

First published in 2023 by Critical Publishing Ltd.

Published 2025 by Routledge
4 Park Square, Milton Park, Abingdon, Oxon OX14 4RN
605 Third Avenue, New York, NY 10017

Routledge is an imprint of the Taylor & Francis Group, an informa business

© 2023 Sarah Alexander

British Library Cataloguing in Publication Data
A CIP record for this book is available from the British Library

ISBN: 9781914171833 (pbk)
ISBN: 9781041057703 (ebk)

Text design by Greensplash
Cover design by Out of House Limited

DOI: 10.4324/9781041057703

Contents

Acknowledgements

I would like to say a heartfelt thank you to my amazing family for their support, patience and encouragement.

I would like to thank Bob Thomson for his support, experience and wisdom and for his brilliant editing. I am very grateful to Critical Publishing for believing in my idea and publishing my first book.

I am thankful to all those I spoke to on the topic of well-being at work for research for this book. I am also grateful to all my clients who I feel privileged to work with. My clients motivate me to continue to learn, grow and develop.

I want to acknowledge The School of Positive Transformation who have so many remarkable teachers in Positive Psychology who taught me and inspired me to apply positive psychology in my work. I am also deeply grateful to the work of Martin Seligman, who proposed the five elements of well-being, the PERMA model. Without his work, this book could not have been written.

Meet the author

Sarah Alexander

I am a highly experienced executive and leadership coach and founder of a successful learning and development consultancy that helps organisations in the UK and internationally develop their people. I am a certified positive psychology practitioner and previously worked for a global healthcare company where I first realised my flair for coaching and developing others. I have a background in science communication which helps me explain positive psychology ideas in engaging and practical ways. I have helped many individuals and teams who want to achieve high performance and want to flourish in what they do – feeling happy and well, with a clear sense of purpose.

Meet the series editor

Bob Thomson

I am a Professor at Warwick Business School, an experienced and accredited coach and supervisor of coaching, and a workplace mediator. I have worked as a volunteer counsellor and as a Samaritan. I am the author of a number of books on coaching and learning from experience as well as series editor for *Business in Mind*.

Introduction

Positivity doesn't simply reflect success and health, it can also produce success and health.

(Fredrickson, 2011)

Positive psychology has the potential to completely transform how people enable high performance in the workplace. Positive psychology is the science of happiness and well-being, the study of how people and communities thrive and flourish. Martin Seligman, the founder of the positive psychology movement, grew frustrated with the emphasis on the negative focus of psychology as a discipline – such as mental illness, trauma and suffering, and how to repair people. He wanted to explore what makes life good, the positive in life, and how to help people move from being OK to actually thriving.

Before the positive psychology movement began in 1998 there were nearly 50,000 scientific papers written on depression in the previous 30 years, and only 400 on happiness. Since then, there has been an amazing growth in the study of happiness. Positive psychologists don't deny that there is suffering and hardship in life; what they say is that we need the positive aspects of ourselves to manage those hardships, and that everyone should be able to welcome happiness and inspiration into their lives. Life and work are about both – stressful times and good times. Positive psychology helps us manage the hard times and thrive in the good times.

Seligman (2011) proposed a model called PERMA, which summarises the key elements that help people to thrive (Table 1.1).

This book explores each aspect of PERMA and how each of them can enable high performance at work as well as enabling well-being. Performance should not be a by-product of well-being at work but an essential component of what it means to be well at work. High performance without consideration for well-being can be effective for a short period, but will likely lead to stress, anxiety and even burnout. Employee burnout was labelled a medical condition by the World Health Organization (WHO) in 2019 with the cause as chronic workplace stress (Pfeffer and Williams, 2020).

There has been an increasing focus on well-being at work, exacerbated by the pandemic that affected so many people physically and emotionally. Many organisations are taking seriously the mental health of their staff, and they are putting in place policies and training that help people feel well at work. Often the focus is still too much on reacting to problems and trying to prevent people going off work with mental health challenges once their health has already deteriorated. Well-being at work is often about helping people to feel 'OK', or to 'manage'. However, when well-being in the workplace is prioritised people should be able to thrive, not just do '*OK*'. A recent survey showed that over 60 per cent of people said their productivity at work was affected by their mental health (Pfeffer and Williams, 2020). Positive psychology interventions help people feel more than just '*OK*' and '*managing*', enabling optimal performance for people and organisations. When people thrive, performance thrives.

Table 1.1 PERMA categories

P	Positive emotions
E	Engagement
R	Relationships
M	Meaning
A	Accomplishment

WELL-BEING AND PERFORMANCE AT WORK

Who is responsible for well-being at work? It is easy to feel that it is the senior leader's responsibility, or those who work in the People/HR department. But there are two groups of people missing here that are absolutely crucial to employee well-being. Line managers are the first group – they are likely to be the first people to notice signs of mental distress, and they are the people who can create an environment of wellness for their reportees. Workloads that are unmanageable and manager style are the leading causes of workplace stress.

Second, individuals. We all have a responsibility to ourselves to help manage our own well-being at work and reach out for support when we need it. To be able to do that people need to feel empowered and able to trust that when they reach out, line managers and senior managers will be able to support them and signpost them, with no fear of shame or stigma. Unfortunately, well-being initiatives often miss the mark as they are removed from the everyday core activities of the business. A survey carried out in 2020 found that only 44 per cent of organisations have a well-being strategy, and 41 per cent still feel their well-being initiatives are reactive rather than proactive. Just 38 per cent of companies are currently providing training for managers in supporting staff with mental health problems (CIPD Survey Report, 2020). A Deloitte study in the UK found that an incredible 86 per cent said that they would '*think twice before offering help to a colleague whose mental health concerned them*' (Deloitte Report, 2020). The McKinsey research shows that that long hours, work/life conflict and high job demands have the same harmful effect on health as second-hand smoke (Pfeffer and Williams, 2020). The same research also showed that 90 per cent of employers said that the pandemic affected the mental health and productivity of their teams.

The Chartered Institute of Professional Development describes workplace well-being as '*an environment that actively promotes a state of contentment*' (CIPD Factsheet, 2022). I find it intriguing that the definition is not bolder. If you look up the meaning of contentment, it says '*a state of happiness and satisfaction*', and the example given is '*he found contentment in living a simple life in the country*'. Contentment is associated with a milder form of quiet, simple happiness. Like a warm bath or a hazy sunny day. For businesses aiming for high financial return, and high performance of their teams, '*contentment*' does not seem to be the right word. Surely, well-being should be about thriving or flourishing – these are adjectives from positive psychology. I propose that well-being at work should be about creating an environment that actively promotes people to thrive. I wonder, if the definition of well-being changed from contentment to thriving, whether this would make the link between well-being and performance so much more explicit and real. A contented employee may feel well and happy, but a thriving employee may feel well, happy *and* motivated. As we want businesses to thrive and grow, surely we want our people to thrive and grow within businesses?

Performance at work is the ability of people to do their jobs well and accomplish their tasks to support the achievement of their organisation's goals. In this book I talk a lot about how positive psychology can help improve performance at work. I use the term '*performance*' generically to mean improving at the tasks that are within your role, responsibilities and objectives, or the tasks within the roles/responsibilities/objectives of the people you lead and manage. Performance is closely linked to productivity, but they are two different concepts. Productivity is a measure of efficiency. So, performance or outcomes could improve in an organisation through people putting in more hours, but this would not improve productivity.

When responsibilities and objectives are closely aligned with the organisation's purpose, then increased performance will equal increased productivity for the business. If the objectives are not particularly aligned with the company goals then it doesn't matter how well the employee does on achieving their objectives, they will not contribute, or contribute little towards an increase in overall productivity for the business. Or if the person is working long hours to reach their level of performance, again this would not improve productivity.

Importantly, the idea of improving performance needs to go hand in hand with realising potential. It is not about being pushed or pushing yourself to achieve unattainable goals or unrealistic workloads. Improving performance using ideas from positive psychology is about how you can achieve more while also feeling good, motivated and well. It is not about doing longer hours to achieve high performance, but using the hours you have in the most productive and positive way you can. Crucially, when we are discussing performance at work, the positive psychology research field has shown conclusively that well-being and happiness *cause* desirable outcomes, they are not just the result of desirable outcomes (Seligman, 2019).

UNDERSTANDING POSITIVE PSYCHOLOGY

In 2000, Seligman and Csikszentmihalyi published 'Positive Psychology: An Introduction', a foundational article in the field of positive psychology that included the new idea that the focus of psychology should not just be about curing the mentally ill, but also about preventing mental illness through helping people to flourish. They said: '*A science of positive subjective experience, positive individual traits, and positive institutions promises to improve quality of life and prevent the pathologies that arise when life is barren and meaningless*' (Seligman and Csikszentmihalyi, 2000).

Positive psychology is first and foremost a science and it is not just '*positive thinking*'. I don't ascribe to '*positive thinking*', as it implies you should disregard negative emotions or thoughts, and ruthlessly or systematically focus on just the positive. From my own experience and working with my many clients in coaching, if you feel or think negatively, the worst thing you can do is to ignore, deny or feel ashamed of the negative thoughts or feelings. The first step to real change is awareness and acceptance. Positive psychologists believe that negativity is just as important as positivity, and you cannot have one without the other, just as you cannot have day without night.

In 2000 Seligman and Csikszentmihalyi proposed that the absence of a mental disorder is not the best that humans could aspire to, that humans can aspire to much more, and that there is value in researching what makes us thrive. Positive psychology is about understanding what makes us feel psychological well, and how being psychologically well enables people to flourish and achieve their goals. In 2011 Seligman proposed his PERMA model: each of the elements supports well-being, can be pursued independently of the other elements for its own sake and is defined independently from the others. There are synergies between all of them, though, and each part of PERMA complements the other elements (Seligman, 2011).

Positive psychology focuses on three different areas, the first being positive experiences: satisfaction and contentment about the past; hope and optimism about the future; and happiness in the present. The second is positive traits such as capacity for love, courage, perseverance, forgiveness and wisdom. The third area is positive institutions including altruism, tolerance and civic virtues.

POSITIVE PSYCHOLOGY INTERVENTIONS

In this book I introduce each element of PERMA and talk about how each part of PERMA increases well-being and performance at work. Each element can increase positive experiences, positive states and increase positivity in an organisation. I also include a chapter specifically on resilience as an extra R, as there are specific positive psychology interventions that help resilience to explore separately from the other five letters. There will also be practical ideas in each chapter based on the insights and reflections that individuals and teams can do.

In each chapter there are some suggested activities or actions based on each element of PERMA. For example, in Chapter 2, where I discuss positive emotions, there are some activities that help increase positive emotions in the workplace that you can do for yourself or with your team. Intentional activities that have the aim of improving well-being (not treating illness) and positive thoughts, feelings and behaviours are called *Positive Psychology Interventions* (PPIs) (Trom and Burke, 2022). PPIs have an encouraging scientific evidence base that shows they are effective in enhancing well-being (Bolier et al, 2013). They can be self-help interventions, interventions with another person (such as coaching or therapy) or interventions with a group or team. Some examples of PPIs are gratitude exercises, exercises to encourage kindness and setting personal goals.

There are established PPIs that are well known in the positive psychology field, such as the Three Good Things exercise. In this exercise, at the end of every day you write down three things that went well for you that day or three things that you are grateful for, and how they make you feel. This focuses your mind on the positive aspects of the day and has been shown to improve well-being. I will include some of the well-known PPIs in this book and suggest some others that are applicable and useful in a work context to transform performance.

I find the ideas from adult development theory really useful when reflecting on how adults change over time as they develop in their careers. There are four forms of mind that adults can hold. The first is a *self-sovereign form of mind*: in this form of mind people find it difficult to understand others' views and actions, they are internally motivated and see others as helpers or blockers. A *socialised form of mind* allows people to take the perspective of other people/ theories/organisations, and they can become embedded in those views, such as becoming embedded in the views of the organisation or team within which they work. The next form is the *self-authored form of mind*, when people can take multiple perspectives and hold their own view. The most developed form of mind is the *self-transforming form of mind*. In this form of mind '*The person sees and understands the perspectives of others and uses those perspectives to continually transform her own system becoming more expansive and more inclusive*' (Garvey Berger, 2012). The highest form of mind understands in life that nothing is and everything is changing all of the time. People with the self-transforming form of mind constantly question assumptions and they see connections that are not visible to others.

Each form of mind is not a growth of skills, but a growth of mind. With each higher form of mind you develop a more complex understanding of the world. Garvey Berger, who has written about adult development in the context of leadership recommends to support the development of form of mind you can do three things. Firstly, ask different questions (ask questions to take other perspectives on situations and increase the capacity to learn), secondly seek multiple perspectives (empathise and understand the views of others even when they are very different to your own) and thirdly see the system (appreciate patterns, connections, trends, habits) (Garvey Berger 2012) The self-coaching questions and practical activities aim to help you consider questions on the topics, reflect on multiple perspectives and think about the system/the bigger picture. They aim to support growth of mind and positive change.

It is really important to me that you come away from reading this with not just ideas, but also some suggestion on how you can actually apply the ideas in the workplace to make positive change for yourself or others. This comes from my deep-rooted belief based on my coaching training and experience that telling adults (and often children!) what to do never leads to sustained or positive change. Positive change and progress come from individual insights and reflections. I also always read a professional book with the question in mind '*what can I apply here?*'. Therefore, I really encourage you to work through the coaching questions at the end of each chapter to think '*what does this really mean for me or my team, or my organisation?*'.

COACHING AND POSITIVE PSYCHOLOGY

Coaching uncovers potential and enables change. Coaching sessions are reflective, open conversations that enable personal growth and improve performance. In coaching the person being coached – the coachee – sets the agenda, and the coach facilitates the discussion, working towards goals that are described by the coachee.

The coach asks questions, uses tools and techniques, uses their experience and provides reflections and observations to enable the coachee to discover within themselves the route to change. Coaching is a perfect partner for positive psychology. Both are based on the idea that by working towards fulfilling your potential you can make positive change in your life and work. *'Positive psychology coaching'* is an approach to coaching that is based on ideas from positive psychology. It is defined as *'enhancement of well-being and perform- ance in personal life and work domains'* (Green and Palmer, 2018). Positive psychology coaching shares some of the characteristics of other types of coaching: the importance of the coach/coachee relationship, the belief that the coachee is resourceful and able to fulfil their potential, and the use of similar conversational tools such as open questions, building awareness and accountability. More generally, in any type of coaching, there is plenty of evidence that shows when people set personally meaningful goals in coaching and they make progress in moving towards them, they subsequently have increased well-being.

At the end of each chapter I have included some self-coaching questions. These questions are included to help you think through how the ideas in the chapter directly relate to you and your work. To do this effectively, let's understand coaching a bit more and the different stages coaching can take you through on a process of change.

Coaching takes the coachee through various stages of discovery, to enable change. The first stage is increasing awareness of what is currently happening without judgement and what you would like to change, the second is being accountable for that change, the third is taking steps to make the change happen and, lastly, appraising what has happened.

Figure 1.1 The 4 As of coaching

1) Awareness

I am able to control only that of which I am aware. That of which I am unaware controls me.

(Whitmore, 2009)

Awareness of yourself

- Your feelings – how do you feel about things currently, how you would like to feel?
- Your thoughts – what are you thinking about it? What first springs to mind?
- Your current actions/behaviours – what are you currently doing, how are you currently behaving?

Awareness of others around you

- Who else influences the situation?
- Who else is involved?
- What do those people think/feel/say about the situation?

Awareness of the situation (what has happened, what is happening, what is likely to happen next)

The facts and information about the situation.

Awareness of the broader situation

Other elements of the situation that may be relevant, such as timing or political or geographical context.

Often awareness gradually comes into focus like an old photograph being developed, or a mirror gradually de-misting. Sometimes awareness can come all at once with a revelation, this is sometimes referred to as an '*aha*' moment of realisation. Often a sudden awareness is referred to as a shock or a surprise, as you were not expecting the answer you have uncovered. Both types of awareness, sudden and gradual, can be the springboard for change.

2) Accountability

Accountability or responsibility is about understanding what you can be accountable for changing and realising that only *you* can make the change. You take the responsibility to do something different.

Accountability means that action is far more likely to happen. If you are only aware but do not take accountability for the action, you cannot make a change. A recent study investigated the effect on outcomes of actions when people were either told what to do, or they decided for themselves. This study particularly investigated what happens when people are coerced into taking a negative action (such as causing pain to another) and how that impacted on their sense of responsibility for the pain.

The study found that people felt less accountable for their actions when they were told what to do. Even brain activity supported the result, with less brain activity when the participants were told, versus when they independently acted (Caspar et al, 2016).

Accountability can be viewed like a seesaw. At one end you have accountable, at the other end you have unaccountable. At some point the seesaw is tipped towards accountable. The seesaw analogy also represents the idea that you cannot be somewhat accountable for an action, or 80 per cent accountable for an action. You are either 100 per cent accountable for an action you will take or you are 0 per cent accountable for an action. (You will either do something different, or you won't do something different.) We sometimes believe that we can be less than 100 per cent accountable to change (it relies on so and so doing this, or the weather being like that, or your work schedule being a certain way, for example). As long as we factor in elements that are out of our control that have an impact on whether we will take action or not, then we won't accept accountability for change.

3) Action

The third stage is action. Action is where change happens. Action can be something that the coachee does outside of the session to make a change. In coaching the coach supports the coachee in deciding what actions they will take; often this is clarified at the end of the session, with the coachee being clear about what actions they will do before the next session.

But action can also happen spontaneously from awareness and accountability, or as a process of change through a coaching conversation. Action can be a change of mindset or thinking patterns, or a change in feelings or a physical change, such as the feeling of a load being lifted from someone's shoulders. Many times in my coaching sessions, I have asked someone near the end of the session what actions they will do or what has changed for them from our discussion. Many people have said '*I feel lighter*', or '*I am already thinking in a different way*'.

Sometimes people will say to me '*I just don't know what to do*', and that is their starting place. The tendency can be to jump to considering actions to solve a problem or manage a difficult situation. This is often where people who self-coach can let their impatience to find a solution not let them spend time on the stages of awareness and accountability. If time is well spent in the first two, the actions needed are so much clearer and more powerful.

Action is not an ending, you don't reach a '*place of action*' (although, of course, specific actions can be completed), you do actions continuously to enable change as we are all changing all of the time, as is our environment, and others around us. Therefore, we need to iteratively do '*action*' so that we can continue to learn, grow and develop.

4) Appraising

There is also a fourth A, although it is really just a specific form of awareness. Appraising is about reviewing what has happened, celebrating what you have achieved and reflecting on how things are different. This A represents an awareness of the new situation, when the cycle of change can begin again. In coaching, appraising happens continuously as coachees reflect on how the changes they are making are having impact. Appraising also happens more formally at the end of a set of coaching sessions. It is useful to get into the habit of reflecting to periodically appraise your own development. I often encourage coachees to ask the simple questions: What is working? What is not working? What would I like to change? This is a simple framework for appraising.

Self-coaching

Self-coaching is a self-reflective practice using coaching tools and techniques to effect a change or improve performance.

Self-coaching is about being able to find the answers within yourself. It is about taking the time out to ask questions of yourself or using tools that you can easily learn and apply in many situations to raise your own awareness. It is like having a map that can guide you to make decisions and make changes, where previously you did not know the route, or even that there was a map available. It is also about forming useful networks that can support you in change.

Self-coaching enables you to step back from your complex system, become aware of repeated, habitual behaviour and use new insights to change parts of the system through careful analysis. To be able to transform performance at work through positive psychology ideas, or indeed to make any positive change, it is important to have a growth mindset. A growth mindset is the belief that your abilities, intelligence, strengths and skills are not fixed – that you have the ability to change and grow and that success comes from effort and hard work. A fixed mindset is the mindset that you cannot change your intelligence or talents, and that success comes from natural ability not through hard work (Dweck, 2017).

Over the last 30 years Carol Dweck, Professor of Psychology at Stanford University, has been studying fixed and growth mindsets, and Dweck coined the term '*growth mindset*'. From her studies she showed that a belief in the ability to grow and change leads to higher achievement. Believing in a growth mindset makes effort worthwhile, which is motivating and therefore self-perpetuating as it leads to more effort and greater performance.

If you have a fixed mindset, you believe that intelligence is static throughout your life, and that toil and training will have little impact. You will also feel that you have to prove yourself all of the time, and that each task ahead of you is a challenge to show how good you are, and you will succeed or fail. You may believe that no matter how hard you try you just will not achieve something. You may say things like:

> *Well, I have never been very good at X and I can't change it.*
> *People like me never have luck.*
> *People like me don't achieve things like that.*
> *People like me will never be really happy.*

You are likely to ignore any negative feedback from others and dismiss it as unhelpful and critical. You will likely find negative feedback very difficult to swallow. You will also probably feel threatened by other people being successful, and it may make you uneasy and envious. You may see others' success as unfair.

Even if some of these behaviours and thoughts sound like you, you can evolve from a fixed mindset to a growth mindset. Dweck says: '*For 20 years, my research has shown that the view you adopt for yourself profoundly affects the way you lead your life. It can determine whether you become the person you want to be and whether you accomplish the things you value*' (Dweck, 2017). Approaching this book and the self-coaching exercises with a growth mindset is the foundation for positive change.

THE GROW TOOL

In this book I encourage you to self-coach on each of the topics we cover. I will introduce you to a coaching tool now that you can use on your own to self-coach, and you can use it to coach others. This coaching tool is called GROW and is possibly the best-known coaching tool; it is certainly one that learner coaches are often introduced to first in their training. It was first developed by John Whitmore, Graham Alexander and Alan Fine in the 1980s and is widely trained to coaches across the world.

GROW can be used to help raise awareness and encourage accountability. Whitmore (2009) says, '*GROW without the context of awareness and responsibility and the skill of questioning to generate them has little value*'.

GROW is an acronym for Goal, Reality, Options, Will. It is a tool that coaches use to structure their discussions with the coachee. The tool helps the coachee to reflect in a structured way, reflecting on different aspects of the situation in a certain order. You can use GROW to self-coach by asking yourself questions about each different aspect.

- **G**oal – helps you decide what you want to achieve.
- **R**eality – explores what is currently going on for you and who and what is involved in the situation.
- **O**ptions – explores options that you can take to move forward.
- **W**ill – narrows down actions to decide those that you will actually take and when.

GROW can be used in any situation where you would like a change to occur. You need time to reflect on the questions, and therefore it is most effective when you have the time and the motivation to think through the answers to the questions. For each element of PERMA there will be a set of GROW questions for you to structure your self-reflection.

SUMMARY CHECKLIST

- Positive Psychology (PP) is the study of how people and communities flourish
- Well-being at work has become an increasingly important focus due to the impact of mental health challenges in the workplace on individuals and on the business
- PP describes five areas that PP can support improved well-being and performance at work through PERMA: increasing positive emotions (P), increasing engagement (E), forming positive relationships (R), finding meaning (M) and having a feeling of accomplishment (A).
- Coaching is a useful tool to enable change through increasing awareness, accountability, action and appraising
- The GROW tool from coaching can be used to self-coach and will be included at the end of each chapter for you to reflect on your own insights and actions to support your performance and well-being at work, and that of others
- Positive Psychology Interventions are intentional activities that have the aim of improving well-being and positive thoughts, feelings and behaviours

REFERENCES

Bolier, L, Haverman, M, Westerhof, G J, Riper, H, Smit, F and Bohlmeijer, E (2013) Positive Psychology Interventions: A Meta-Analysis of Randomized Controlled Studies. *BMC Public Health*, 13: 119. [online] Available at: www.biomedcentral.com/1471-2458/13/119 (accessed 3 March 2023).

Caspar, E A, Christensen, J F, Cleeremans, A and Haggard, P (2016) Coercion Changes the Sense of Agency in the Brain. *Current Biology*, 26(5): 585–92.

CIPD Survey Report (2020) Health and Wellbeing at Work. [online] Available at: www.cipd.co.uk/Images/health-and-well-being-2020-report_tcm18-73967.pdf (accessed 3 April 2023).

CIPD Factsheet (2022) Wellbeing at Work. [online] Available at: www.cipd.co.uk/knowledge/culture/well-being/factsheet#gref (accessed 3 March 2023).

Deloitte Report (2020) Mental Health and Employment. [online] Available at: www2.deloitte.com/uk/en/pages/consulting/articles/mental-health-and-employers-refreshing-the-case-for-investment.html (accessed 3 April 2023).

Dweck, C (2017) *Mindset*. New York: Random House.

Fredrickson, B (2011) *Positivity*. London: Oneworld.

Garvey Berger, J (2012) *Changing on The Job*. Stanford, CA: Stanford University Press.

Green, S and Palmer, S (2018) *Positive Psychology Coaching in Practice*. London and New York: Routledge.

Pfeffer, J and Williams, L (2020) Mental Health in the Workplace: The Coming Revolution. *McKinsey Quarterly*. [online] Available at: www.mckinsey.com/industries/healthcare-systems-and-services/our-insights/mental-health-in-the-workplace-the-coming-revolution (accessed 3 March 2023).

Seligman, M E P (2011) *Flourish*. London: Nicholas Brealey Publishing.

Seligman, M E P (2019) Positive Psychology: A Personal History. *Annual Review of Clinical Psychology*, 15: 1–23. [online] Available at: https://motamem.org/wp-content/uploads/2021/06/seligman-positive-psychology-a-personal-history.pdf (accessed 3 March 2023).

Seligman, M E P and Csikszentmihalyi, M (2000) Positive Psychology: An Introduction. *American Psychologist*, 55(1): 5–14. doi: 10.1037/0003-066X.55.1.5.

Trom, P and Burke, J (2022) Positive Psychology Intervention (PPI) Coaching: An Experimental Application of Coaching to Improve the Effectiveness of Gratitude Intervention. *Coaching: An International Journal of Theory, Research and Practice*, 15(1): 131–42. doi:10.1080/17521882.2021.1936585.

Whitmore, J (2009) *Coaching for Performance*. Boston: Nicholas Brealey Publishing.

2 Happy high performer

These fleeting states are remarkably fragile yet somehow they add up to a power to change the very course of our lives

(Fredrickson, 2011)

POSITIVE EMOTIONS

This chapter explains the power of positive emotions, the P (positive emotions) of PERMA, and how they can broaden and build our capacity to perform at work. Positive psychology is dedicated to understanding happiness and positive experiences in life; therefore, how to increase positive, happy emotions is a central theme. Yet, positive emotions do not just make us feel good, they also make us do good and do more. The chapter explores how integral they are to well-being and flourishing and explains how to increase your own positive emotions and those of others in a way that enables an upward spiral. Positive emotions are like potent sparks of energy, a powerful engine, driving personal and team well-being and performance.

An emotion is derived from circumstances, mood or relationships with others. It is a state brought on by changes in our nervous system (neurophysiological changes). Emotions are a response to internal or external events that result in a behavioural response that you can often see on the outside, such as a smile, laugh, tears or a frown. Importantly, emotions are temporary; that is why they are referred to as a state. A state is the particular condition that someone or something is in at a specific time. Emotions are not meant to last indefinitely.

It is fascinating to consider how we talk about emotions: '*I just want to* be *happy*' or I am going to 'become *angry*'. We actually talk about becoming the emotion. While we may self-identify as that emotion ('*I am a happy person*'), we don't really become the emotion; the emotion is a state that we feel for a short, or sometimes longer, period of time. '*Being*' happy is actually *feeling* happy emotions frequently. This idea is crucial when considering a mindset of positivity. To increase our own positive emotions, we therefore need to increase the chances of having them with the aim of increasing their frequency. At the same time, we need to be aware and comfortable with the idea that positive emotions will come and go. In the workplace, to increase well-being and performance through the lever of positive emotions, individuals and teams need to have plenty of opportunities to experience positive feelings about their work and with their colleagues.

You are likely to have experienced the impact of feeling good at work: leaving a meeting that has inspired you to push on with a project; laughing with colleagues and then feeling uplifted and able to get on with the job; sipping a much-needed coffee and getting into the detail of a report; chatting with a colleague and then having some fresh ideas.

You are also likely to have experienced the opposite: a day when you felt low, tired, sad or angry. The overly long meeting that reduced your motivation from a novel to a postcard, the harsh negative feedback delivered abruptly by your manager that dried out your enthusiasm, or the difficult stakeholder or customer who always finds fault with your work and impacts your focus and purpose.

In my coaching practice I have seen the impact of people feeling happier at work and how that drives their motivation, focus and energy.

Importantly, becoming a happy high performer, who feels well and performs at their best, is not about eliminating all negative emotions and thoughts. Negative emotions give us a contrast to positive emotions; without the negative it is harder to appreciate the good. Negative emotions have a key evolutionary purpose; they encourage us to act in ways that boost our chances of survival. They prime us for reaction from fear of a threat or anger to attack (fight or flight). An element of pressure in the workplace also leads to heightened performance (Fredrickson, 2001). 'Good' stress, as opposed to chronic stress, has been shown to increase creativity in employees when the pressure was viewed as a challenge, rather than a hindrance – such as some time pressure, sizeable workload and varied responsibilities. Kashdan and Biswas-Diener (2015) show how they see negative emotions as motivators to help us address and correct behaviour and take action. This is crucial, as the importance of positive emotions to drive performance does not mean creating a purely comfortable, utopian space where teams live in an idealistic comfort zone, feeling well and happy. Truly top performance is about feeling good while also embracing challenges, pressures, risks and ambitious goals (Kashdan and Biswas-Diener, 2015; Ren and Zhang, 2015). Top performers know and welcome the idea that we need to sometimes feel negative emotions, such as nerves or pressure, to drive and motivate us. Who hasn't worked harder as a key deadline approaches, when the adrenalin kicks in and the pressure builds?

Therefore, you need both positive and negative emotions, but in what proportion?

Research has been carried out in this area, most notably by Losada (1999), who proposed that the ratio 3:1 positive to negative emotions over the course of a day was indicative of flourishing. While the calculations that led to this exact figure have been questioned, it is clear that the higher the ratio of positive emotions to negative emotions, the more likely it is that you will flourish (Fredrickson, 2013).

IMPROVING WELL-BEING

So how do our positive emotions improve our well-being? From the first chapter you will know that well-being is about feeling comfortable, happy and healthy. An individual at work with high well-being will feel comfortable in their role, happy with their day-to-day responsibilities and well enough physically and mentally to do their job. A team with high well-being will feel comfortable with their team purpose, they will enjoy working together and they will feel well enough to mentally and physically support each other and achieve their team vision.

At the simplest level positive emotions partner with the chemicals in our brain and messages in our nervous system to make us feel good. Positive emotions enable and are enabled by the release of particular hormones and chemicals into our blood stream that manage and maintain happy feelings (Dale and Peyton, 2019).

The absence of positive emotions over time and the increase of negative emotions such as anxiety, helplessness, anger or frustration at work can lead to work-related stress. Work-related stress has a wide-ranging impact on work relationships, mental and physical health, behaviour and performance.

> The Health and Safety Executive Report (2022) shows 17.9 million days were lost due to work-related stress, depression or anxiety in Great Britain from 2021 to 2022. That is likely to be an underestimate as some people will blame their days away from the office on something else.

The numbers also reflect the increased stress and anxiety caused by the Covid-19 pandemic. Chronic stress leads to physical (such as headaches, stomach aches, high heart rate), behavioural (such as shouting or crying), cognitive (forgetfulness, lack of focus and indecision) and emotional (such as anxiety, fear or boredom) symptoms (Pfeffer and Williams, 2020). Therefore, positive emotions are crucial in well-being not just for enabling enjoyment in the moment but also as the frequency of experiencing them causes changes in the body that lead to decreased probability of chronic stress and other physical illnesses.

They are also integral to our ability to manage difficulties and our ability to cope through tough times and recover from stressful events (Ong et al, 2006). A colleague at work making you smile or laugh during a stressful period will lead to mood-enhancing hormones flooding through your body, enabling quicker recovery from a difficult time. Chapter 7 looks in more detail at how ideas from positive psychology can help us to be more resilient, and positive emotions are a part of that.

So, we know that positive emotions affect us physiologically and that leads us to feel more positive in the moment. Initially, Martin Seligman – who is considered the father of positive psychology – proposed that happy feelings from doing things we enjoy, that give us pleasure, are merely the first step towards happiness. That, on its own, pleasure is nice, but easily overdosed on, and not nearly as important as other areas of positive psychology. Research from Barbara Fredrickson (Fredrickson, 2011) on positive emotions makes it clear that a transient moment of feeling good is just scratching the surface of what positive emotions do for us. A smile or laugh, or any outward sign of positivity, make the workplace a more pleasant place to be in that specific moment of enjoyment, *and* each micro-moment of happiness builds over time to create a cumulative force that builds well-being.

Positive emotions also create motives we are not aware of for continuing with wellness behaviours, such as running or eating healthily, which lead to a happy upward spiral of lifestyle change (Fredrickson and Joiner, 2018). The reasons that motivate us to change to healthier behaviours, such as having enough of feeling lethargic, or wanting to *not* be overweight, are not usually the reasons we continue with a new healthy behaviour. What determines whether we continue (with healthier eating, for example, or a new exercise plan) is largely whether we are gaining enjoyment from the new behaviour – is it giving us pleasure? This is the immediate reward (Woolley and Fishbach, 2016). If something is not enjoyable, then we are likely to let it peter out. This explains the packed gyms in January, and the empty ones in March. The more people enjoy something the more likely they are to have spontaneous thoughts about it, and therefore engage in it again. When we dread something, even if it is good for us, we are far less likely to engage in it frequently.

IMPROVING PERFORMANCE: BROADEN AND BUILD

The hidden power of positive emotions is that they don't just make us feel good in the moment, they fundamentally alter the way that our brains work in that specific moment and over time. In that moment, our brain opens like a flower in response to the sun. This *'opening up'* means that we have a broader awareness of what is going on around us and more awareness of our own connectedness to others. Brain imaging, eye tracking and behavioural studies have all shown this to be true – positive emotions broaden our perspective, and this has powerful benefits for performance at work (Fredrickson, 2001; Rowe et al, 2007; Wadlinger and Isaacowitz, 2006). The Broaden and Build theory of positive emotions proposed by Barbara Fredrickson demonstrates how our emotions are far more potent in improving performance than previously thought.

> *Evidence confirms that positive emotions broaden thought-action repertoires: induced positive emotions produce wider visual search patterns, novel and creative thoughts and actions, more inclusive social groups, and more flexible goals and mindsets.*

> (Cohn et al, 2009)

Skills that are becoming increasingly important in the modern workplace are enhanced by positive emotions. The Future of Jobs report (World Economic Forum, 2020) lists the top skills that will be needed in the workplace in 2025. Several among the top 15 are enhanced by positive emotions: innovation, complex problem solving, creativity, social influence, resilience, persuasion and emotional intelligence (of which empathy is a key component).

Let's explore these a bit more. First, through the brain changing as a consequence of a happy feeling we become more creative and innovative. Fredrickson (2011) illustrates this point with a simple experiment, asking people to brainstorm ideas for future plans after either a) looking at the back of their own hand or b) after imagining a recent joyful occasion. The result, and the result of other substantial research experiments, show that positive emotions lead to more creativity. When people were asked to reflect on negative experiences, their creativity narrowed. By inducing a positive or negative state, individuals and teams can be either opened up or closed down to ideas and innovation. Make people feel good at work and they will have more creative and innovative ideas.

Negative emotions have the opposite effect on the brain, closing down options, and specific negative emotions are usually related to specific actions (for example, fear means to run, anger means to fight/argue) (Tooby and Cosmides, 2000). Positive emotions do not have this direct correlation of an action-specific tendency. Therefore, joy or contentment can lead to different actions, but all positive emotions lead to a broadening rather than narrowing of possible actions. How many times have you heard someone who is feeling down say, '*I just don't know what to do*', or '*I can't see a way forward*'. The way forward often only becomes clear when a positive emotion such as hope or faith is seeded.

Through the broadening of the mind in response to a positive emotion, we also become more empathetic (Fredrickson, 2011). In the many years that I have helped people through coaching to accelerate their careers and their teams' or business' performance, a key theme has emerged. When individuals try to achieve their highest goals on their own *despite* others, rather than *with* others, difficulties always emerge. People live and work in a network. People come to coaching wanting to make change happen, and they realise that change happens inside of them, but it must also happen in the way they build relationships with their networks. Clients want to understand how to change others, and they may say, '*What can I say to them to make them do something different?*' '*How can I improve my communication with them to make the impact I need to have?*' '*How can I influence others to want to work with me, or invest in my business, or give me that next role?*'

Better questions for them to ask are: '*How can I understand others so that I can relate to them in the best way?*' '*How can I understand the network that person/team/business operates in and engage in that network in the best way?*' These questions are better because they lead to increased empathy. The root of understanding others and being able to move others is empathy. Positive emotions broaden our minds to be more empathetic. Strong empathic relationships lead to empowered and trusted teams.

Linked to the notion of increasing empathy is the ability of positive emotions to help us to see the bigger picture. Joy and contentment, two distinct positive emotions, have been shown in studies to increase people's ability to see a situation more broadly – be able to zoom out from the detail to see context. Further studies have shown they help us to be more flexible, be able to negotiate better – perhaps this is linked to increased empathy and seeing the bigger picture – and be more creative in finding solutions in difficult situations. Feeling positive also means we take more care in making decisions and we tend to be more accurate.

Table 2.1 Power of positive emotions to improve performance

See the big picture
Be more flexible
Negotiate better
Take more care in making decisions
Be more accurate

(Fredrickson, 2001; Murray et al, 1990; Carnevale and Isen, 1986; Isen et al, 1987.)

Therefore, positive emotions do not just make us feel good in that fleeting moment: they are the building blocks for our ability to succeed at work by changing our cognitive function – the way that our brains work.

As mentioned earlier, the frequency of feeling positive is key to well-being and performance:

> … the broaden-and-build theory posits that momentary experiences of mild, everyday positive emotions broaden people's awareness in ways that, over time and with frequent recurrence, build consequential personal resources that contribute to their overall emotional and physical well-being. Through incremental broaden-and-build processes, then, positive emotions both open the mind and nourish the growth of resources.

(Fredrickson and Joiner, 2018)

All of this gives us a significant '*why*' for increasing positive emotions. It's not the fluffy stuff, it's the real power behind progress.

So how can we increase our own or others positive emotions to experience all of these benefits in the workplace? Can it be forced? According to Fredrickson, sustained happiness must be heartfelt, not forced. Forced positivity can be damaging. Studies have been done to understand what is happening at the physiological level, such as measuring cortisol (a stress hormone), when people put on a smile to get through hard times but are not feeling happiness inside. The studies show that pretending to be happy has no impact on the stressful changes happening inside, and in some cases make the physiological changes worse.

This is a useful insight when considering what to do to increase well-being and performance at work – imagine the team being forced to do team-building activities and smile through it when they do not enjoy that type of event; or imagine the person who dreads the ice breaker at a team meeting. On a personal level and as a manager or leader of people, it is useful to know that forcing positivity does not work. Finding out what really makes you and others feel positive emotions, even through difficult times, is where the true magic lies.

> There is no quick fix to feeling good. False positive emotions are just a mask that you can wear that will eventually irritate the face and prevent you or your team from flourishing. Positive emotions need to be real and authentic. We must therefore induce *real* happy feelings and understand ourselves and our teams enough to know how to do that.

GROWING POSITIVE EMOTIONS IN THE WORKPLACE

We now look at some practical tools and techniques that you can use for yourself and for others that harness the power of happy feelings and increase positive emotions.

Positive emotions and goals

Imagine a goal to be '*more happy at work*' or '*feel more positive*'. Aiming to '*feel more positive*' is a tricky goal to have, and this is true at a team and organisational level: '*a more positive team*', '*a happier organisation*'. Having such a vague goal means the actions needed to get there are difficult to ascertain. '*Happy*' as an umbrella positive emotion is therefore hard to work with and difficult to aim for.

Martin Seligman (2002) himself said, '*What is happiness anyway?*' *More words have been penned about defining happiness than almost any other philosophical question. I could fill the rest of these pages with just a fraction of the attempts to take this promiscuously overused word and make sense of it.*' Seligman proposes it is much more useful to understand the constituents of happiness, which include the individual positive emotions.

In my own experience from coaching, when a client would like to feel happier in their job, before we even explore options to get there, the conversation must include: What exactly does the client want to feel? What type of happy? What positive emotion? And how will they know that they got there? The client may say, '*I would like to feel more content and less pressured*'. Another client may say, '*I would like to be more interested in my work and have pride in what I do*'. A third may say, '*I want my team to feel confident and trusted*'. A fourth, '*I want my organisation to have a culture of optimism and altruism*'.

Before we look to increase positive emotions at work it is therefore useful to appreciate the spectrum of different positive emotions that we can feel individually and as a team. The top ten most common positive emotions have been categorised as:

1. joy;
2. gratitude;
3. serenity;
4. interest;
5. hope;
6. pride;
7. amusement;
8. inspiration;
9. awe;
10. love.

In the case of 'love' in the workplace, it is about the feeling of caring and warmth towards others.

A longer list of positive emotions from lower energy to higher energy is:

- serenity;
- relief;
- contentment;
- satisfaction;
- gratitude;
- affection;
- hope;
- admiration;
- awe;
- confidence;
- pride;
- inspiration;
- altruism;
- cheerfulness;
- amusement;
- confidence;
- interest;
- love;
- enjoyment;
- optimism;
- excitement;
- surprise;
- eagerness;
- enthusiasm;
- joy;
- euphoria.

While this is a fairly comprehensive list of positive emotions in English, there are some terms in other languages that I love. For example: *fargin* (Yiddish) is to glow with pride at the success of others; *santosha* (Sanskrit) is contentment arising from personal interactions; *seijaku* (Japanese) is serenity in the midst of chaos; and *gjensynsglede* (Norwegian), described as '*goodbye happiness*', is the joy of meeting someone you haven't seen for a long time (Lomas, 2016). Are there others that you would want to include in your list? If you could invent a word to describe a made-up positive emotion, what would it be? (Mine would be *winspired* – when you are brimming with energy and enthusiasm with brilliant, winning ideas!)

When you can recognise what positive emotions would be useful for you, your team or your organisation, then enabling positive changes becomes much more straightforward. For example, if you identify that you would like to feel more optimism at work, that would lead to a very different action plan compared to wanting to feel more confident.

INDIVIDUAL PPI (POSITIVE PSYCHOLOGY INTERVENTION)

- Rank all the positive emotions listed below (first to tenth) with the one you usually experience the most in first place, and then moving down the list to the one you experience the least in tenth place.
- Which ones on your ranked list would you like to increase (feel more of)?
- For those that you would like to increase – what could you do differently at work to feel more of that emotion?

Emotion	Rank
Amusement	
Awe	
Gratitude	
Hope	
Inspiration	
Interest	
Joy	
Love	
Pride	
Serenity	

TEAM PPI (POSITIVE PSYCHOLOGY INTERVENTION)

- Ask your team to each individually draw some happy high performer art. This means ignoring your immediate response of '*I can't draw*', taking a piece of paper and pen(s), and drawing what a happy day at work would look like. Each individual does a drawing, then shares with a partner to explain their drawing. The partner can ask, '*What is in your happy day art that we could actually do today or over the next week?*'.
- As a group you can also have fun with this activity by asking someone to guess what another team member might have drawn and sketching out and seeing how close the guess was. The picture helps inform what your goal as an individual or as a team should be (to ensure that the picture is true on as many days as possible).
- As a team you can also use the spectrum of positive emotions of low energy to high energy and understand which ones your team experience most often and whether there is a good mix of low energy and high energy emotions. A mix of low and high emotions is ideal.

Enhance positivity resonance

Positivity resonance is momentary connections of high-quality communication between people. The momentary connections have three features:

1. shared positivity such as laughing or smiling together, and it is amplified if the other persons shows genuine enthusiasm for you and your thoughts or ideas;
2. mutual care and concern for each other in that moment – responding and not making the other person feel judged;
3. shared behaviours, for example mirrored body language, vocal tone or eye contact.

Sharing positivity in this way amplifies the positive emotions for all involved. This is a great way to nurture your own positivity by actively looking to share positive moments with others at work, and also to grow the positivity of others.

This is not just relevant for the people with whom we work closely. While it is easier to have trust and genuine warmth with people we know, positivity resonance is possible even with strangers. The '*outer circle*' of our social network or '*weak ties*' have a great impact on our daily well-being (Granovetter, 1973). This means saying hello to the person on the desk as you arrive, talking to the new colleague who just arrived but won't be in your team, making an effort to meet the eyes of the person serving you dinner in the canteen – all of these micro moments of connection drive increased positive emotions in the workplace. What we lost through lockdowns during the pandemic was the opportunity to interact with an outer circle of acquaintances and friends, leading to fewer opportunities for positivity resonance.

With increased shared positive emotions people shift their view of others and see more interconnectedness, instead of '*me*' and '*you*', it becomes '*we*' and '*us*'. This drives team spirit and team connectedness. '*Positivity and Trust feed on each other. As our positivity grows, so does our trust in others and vice-versa*' (Fredrickson, 2011).

Why is it that after a team building day there is more laughter and easy conversation than on other days? This is positivity resonance based on communication about the activities the team did the day before.

You can plan for at least one definite positive interaction among a sea of other tasks. This will greatly increase how positive you will feel during the day. For example, schedule a phone call with a colleague who you always have successful meetings with, or a coffee with a colleague who always uplifts you. Plan one certain positive encounter into every workday, and the effects will seep into every subsequent meeting, conversation and even email correspondence. The positive encounter does not have to be at the very start of the day, as the anticipation of something positive will also have a positive effect even before the event.

TOP TIPS FOR INCREASING POSITIVITY RESONANCE AT WORK

- Have a shared positivity section on the team meeting agenda – this could be to share good news, achievements, a humorous happening, a success story.
- Put as much energy and emphasis on positive internal communication as you do on positive external communication.
- Identify believing mirrors – people who always show genuine interest and concern for you and motivate you. Schedule time in your diary to speak to them on a regular basis, especially through difficult times.
- Bring people together in an online event if they are working virtually and ensure regular communication.
- Designate '*happy high performer days*' when there is a focus on sharing positive emotions with others.
- Disengage from conversations with colleagues that involve contempt, hateful sarcasm, blame and criticism of a person (rather than that person's behaviour). These are landmine dialogues.

Use positive language

It takes longer to understand a sentence that uses a negative approach than it does to understand a positive sentence (Haase et al, 2019). For example: '*I don't doubt that he is unwell*' (negative) versus '*I believe that he is unwell*' (positive). Your choice of words is powerful and can be perceived as negative or positive by the listener or the reader. By choosing to use more positive language, the messages you convey will be received more favourably, even when you are communicating bad news. Your language is constructive when you choose positive words over negative words. Positive language can soften a message, persuade people to agree with you, influence others and enable better working relationships. This is important in face-to-face communications but even more so in written communications where your body language or tone cannot soften the language. Using positive language enables you to build stronger relationships in a single moment, and over time to create ripples of positive emotion across your organisation.

'*The right words spoken in the right way can bring us love, money and respect. While the wrong words, or even the right words spoken in the wrong way – can lead a country to war*' (Newberg and Waldman, 2012). Your choice of words is so important because everything you say to others – either spoken or written – is feedback for those you are communicating with. We tend to consider feedback as being something we give to others for their development at work, or for specific thoughts on something someone has said or done. But feedback is given far more frequently than that. Feedback is given all the time by you, by the way you communicate with other people. All your communications to them are your feedback to them.

To speak more positively there are certain words to avoid. The first commonly used negative word is '*But*'. '*I have finished the project but …*'; '*You were great in the meeting, but I thought you should have made that last point earlier on*'. The '*but*' part of the sentence negates the first part.

'*But*' is often used after '*yes*'. '*Yes, but …*'. No one remembers the '*yes*'; they just remember the '*but*'.

You can replace '*but*' with '*and*' – which results in the message being seen as more positive. '*You led that project really well, and you have some development areas in managing conflict.*' '*The meeting was very constructive, and we still have a lot of work to do on the project.*'

It makes the two parts of the sentence seem evenly emphasised. With a '*but*' the second part is construed as being dominant.

Although using '*and*' may seem unnatural at first, it becomes natural with practice, and sounds natural to the listener. The only time to use '*but*' is when the second part of the sentence is positive. '*You made some mistakes, but overall you were brilliant.*'

Other words that have a similar effect are '*unfortunately*' (which is often used with '*but*'): '*I enjoyed the project, but unfortunately …*'. '*Unfortunately*' is often used in writing and '*However*'. Instead of '*however*', or '*but*' or '*unfortunately*', you can use '*and*'.

Other negative phrases often used in writing and sometimes in speech include:

- you failed to include;
- you state that;
- you claim that;
- you must;
- you should;
- no doubt.

You can give negative messages a positive tone by:

- focusing on what can be done;
- avoiding unnecessary negative language if possible, such as *'can't'*, *'won't'* and *'but'*;
- suggesting alternatives if something is not possible;
- explaining positive consequences if certain steps are taken.

Plan positive events

Pleasures are activities we do that make us feel good with a clear sensory response. Pleasures include great food, reading, dancing, watching films and other hobbies. In the workplace planning positive events helps increase positive emotions. For example, team lunches, gifts or prizes for great performance, team build days with activities people enjoy, wellness baskets delivered to people who are having a difficult time.

While these activities are valuable in increasing positive emotion, they also come with a caution. The nature of pleasures is that if they are frequently repeated then this results in habituation. Habituation is your own body and mind adapting to the pleasure and getting less pleasure from it over time. For example, if you always have a treat lunch, then the lunch is no longer so much of a treat but a habit. Some activities you want to become habits – exercising, eating healthily, getting enough sleep, reducing alcohol, getting out in nature. All of these activities, while giving us pleasure, also give us many accumulated benefits from being habitual, and that habitation is desirable. Pleasures such as treat food, team days out, champagne, gift vouchers you should keep as *'treats'* so their power to make you feel more positive remains strong, and the level at which you originally experienced them is enough. (Plus, there is the negative impact on health and wealth for some of these treats such as champagne every day – not the best idea for your liver, brain or bank balance!)

The second caution is that pleasures are sometimes heightened by the element of surprise. Seligman says: *'Surprise as well as spacing keeps pleasures from habituating'*. He also points out that giving nice surprises to others is *'reciprocally contagious'* (Seligman, 2002). This means, for example, that if you surprise colleagues with a cup of coffee or cake, they will want to do the same back for you, creating positive energy and more opportunities for positivity resonance.

Savour the good

While positive emotions are fleeting states, we can learn to savour them – a bit like sucking a sweet for a longer time to continue the enjoyment or eating a lovely meal slowly to enjoy the flavours. Seligman says:

> These techniques all support the four kinds of savouring: basking (receiving praise and congratulations); thanksgiving (expressing gratitude for blessings); marvelling (losing the self in the wonder of the moment); and luxuriating (indulging the senses).

(Seligman, 2002)

TOP TIPS FOR SAVOURING POSITIVE FEELINGS

- Seek out others to share the positive experience you had and explain to them how much you value that positive experience – sharing with others is a key way to savour positive emotions.
- Help yourself to remember positive events or feelings by keeping physical moments from the experience, or by focusing on details that you can see, hear or feel during the positive experience. For example, if you are having a one-to-one with your manager and they give you some great feedback from a stakeholder, pause for a moment to remember what the stakeholder said, how you feel and what you are seeing. It is like painting a picture or making a drawing of all the things around you as you have that positive experience.
- Give yourself positive feedback and congratulate yourself if things go well. The ability to give yourself feedback both positive and negative, and not be reliant on constant external feedback to feel confident, is a key skill of a leader.
- Create a smile file in your emails or messages and file positive emails/messages in it to look back on when you are feeling down.
- Be in the moment, allow yourself to be immersed in something positive without worrying about the next challenge. For example, if you were having a team meeting and you wanted to celebrate a recent success, let the meeting be about the success, allow the team to be absorbed momentarily in the good. Don't end the meeting with '*what's next*', or looking at a further challenge. Give good time and focus to what is positive.

Increase gratitude

The reason gratitude works to increase life satisfaction is that it amplifies good memories about the past, their intensity, their frequency and the tag lines the memories have.

(Seligman, 2002)

Gratitude helps us to feel more positive emotions by selectively choosing to think about what is good. Gratitude is a positive emotion that is about noticing and appreciating something or being thankful for it. Gratitude also helps cement working relationships, and research on gratitude proposes that the emotion has actually evolved to help foster good relationships: '*[gratitude] evolved to help solve a central problem of human survival: identifying high-quality relationship partners and keeping them interested in the relationship*' (Algoe et al, 2016).

TOP TIPS FOR INCREASING GRATITUDE IN THE WORKPLACE

- At the end of every working week write down three things you are grateful for from that week.
- Share three things you are grateful for that you have done with your team each week/month.
- Share things you are grateful for with team members in one-to-ones.
- Hunt for the good in everything. Even hard times make us stronger, as we will explore in the chapter on resilience. What can you be grateful for from a difficult period at work?
- When you feel happy, name the emotion in your head (such as '*I feel joy*', or '*I feel contentment*') and be thankful for feeling it. The act of naming the emotion helps you to focus on it.
- Plan ahead and ask yourself what three things you would like you or your team to be thankful for at the end of the week (what we focus on grows).
- Give positive feedback to others when it is deserved, and tell them why the action mattered ('*I noticed X and this meant Y*').
- Recognise and reward great achievement for others and for yourself.

INDIVIDUAL PPI

Gratitude exercise

- Designate one day/week as your day to focus on being grateful.
- Spend three minutes in the morning, before you open your emails/messages or start any work, writing down three things you are grateful for about the week ahead. Make sure you take the time to write them down or type them as this helps you focus.
- Build in as many opportunities to show gratitude during that day. Ideas: thank a colleague, write a thank you note, send out team thanks, give some positive feedback to yourself and to others, reflect on what is going well at work, look back over any previous good feedback you have been given.
- After doing this for four weeks, ask yourself, what parts of my weekly gratitude day could I do on a daily basis?

TEAM PPI

The feedback challenge

This is a fun energetic challenge that builds gratitude.

Gather the team in a large room and get everyone to stand on their own around the room. Ask them to find someone in the room to pair with. When they reach their pair, they need to give each other one piece of positive feedback. They have two minutes to do this, then they must find someone else in the room and form a new pair and give another piece of positive feedback. Do five rounds of the feedback giving. Ask the team to use the format: *'I noticed X, and when you do X it means Y'*, so that the positive feedback is given in a way that says what is positive and outlines the impact that positive action has.

SUMMARY CHECKLIST

How to increase positive emotions in the workplace

- Have clear positive goals.
- Enhance positivity resonance.
- Use positive language in speech and writing.
- Savour the good whenever possible.
- Increase gratitude on a daily basis.

REFLECTIONS

Perhaps you have read this chapter and reflected that, yes, you would like to increase positive emotions at work, but because the environment or culture at your workplace is not positive, then nothing you can do will make things better. Of course, it is possible that you need to change role or organisation if you are experiencing low positive emotions which are impacting your well-being and your performance. But leaving may not be possible, or you may not want to leave because of a host of reasons such as career progression, renumeration, the flexibility or locality of the role. One of the books that has had the most impact on me is Viktor Frankl's testimony from his experiences in a concentration camp, *Man's Search for Meaning* (2004). While I am in no way suggesting a workplace could parallel Frankl's experience, the ideas in the book are relevant. His experiences clearly show that you can be in the most hellish place possible, and yet still find friendship, hope, faith and even humour.

Positive emotions can seed anywhere. A mindset of having the option of and choosing to be positive even in the darkest hour is a powerful realisation. This is a crucial concept at work because we can often believe that things outside of us have to change for us to feel happy. '*If only I could finish earlier*', '*If only my manager understood me better*', '*If only I my colleagues could change their habits*', then I will feel happy.

When I am working with clients a really useful exercise to is map out what is in their control, what they can influence, and what is out of their influence or control, or they have very little influence over.

One of my clients put their anger as out of their control. Clearly, as long as that belief was held onto, anger would always be part of their working day. With awareness that anger is an internal response to either internal or external triggers, and that our responses can be chosen, the person came to realise that anger can move inwards to influence and possibly in time move further to control. This is possible for all of the positive emotions discussed in this chapter – choosing to feel them. This does not mean accepting injustice or poor conditions or being passive when there are difficult times at work. What it does mean is taking responsibility for your own thoughts, feelings and behaviours and knowing that what you focus on grows. By focusing on how to increase your own and others' positivity at work through doing the activities in this chapter you will grow your positive emotions and others' positive emotions and reap all the benefits that brings to your well-being and performance at work.

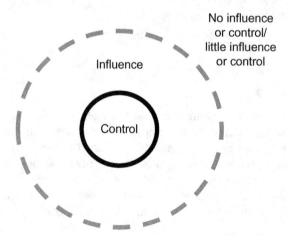

Figure 2.1 Mapping influence

SELF-COACHING QUESTIONS

As explained in Chapter 1, you can use the GROW model to structure your self-reflections and coach yourself and others (individuals or teams). Work through GROW for this topic and do add more questions/reflections at each stage than are detailed here if you want to explore further.

Goal (to uncover what your aim is)

- What specifically would I like to improve with regards to:
    - my positive emotions?
    - my team's positive emotions?
    - the culture in my organisation regarding positivity?

Reality (to understand)

- What is going on for me that makes this something I would like to change?
- What is going on for my team that makes this something I would like to change?
- How often do I feel positive emotions at work?
- How often do my team members share positive moments with each other?
- How often do the teams across my organisation share positive moments together?

Options (to explore)

- What could I do to increase positivity at work for myself and for my team?
- Who, apart from myself, needs to make a change in my team?
- How can I influence others to make a change?
- If I woke up tomorrow and my goal had been reached, what would be the first thing I would notice that was different?

Will (to decide on action)

- What actions will I take?
- What deadlines will I set for myself?
- How will I know things have changed?

REFERENCES

Algoe, S, Kurtz, L E and Hilaire, N M (2016) Putting the 'You' in 'Thank You': Examining Other-Praising Behavior as the Active Relational Ingredient in Expressed Gratitude. *Social Psychological and Personality Science*, 7(7): 658–66.

Carnevale, P J D and Isen, A M (1986) The Influence of Positive Affect and Visual Access on the Discovery of Integrative Solutions in Bilateral Negotiation. *Organizational Behavior and Human Decision Processes*, 37(1):1–13.

Cohn, M, Fredrickson, B, Brown, S, Mikels, J and Conway, A (2009) Happiness Unpacked: Positive Emotions Increase Life Satisfaction by Building Resilience. *Emotion*, 9(3): 361–8. doi: 10.1037/a0015952.

Dale, C and Peyton, P (2019) *Physical Intelligence*. London: Simon and Schuster.

Deloitte (2012) Core Beliefs and Culture. [online] Available at: www2.deloitte.com/content/dam/Deloitte/global/Documents/About-Deloitte/gx-core-beliefs-and-culture.pdf (accessed 6 March 2023).

Frankl, V (2004) *Man's Search for Meaning*. London: Penguin Random House.

Fredrickson, B (2001) The Role of Positive Emotions in Positive Psychology. The Broaden-and-Build Theory of Positive Emotions. *American Psychologist*, 56(3): 218–26.

Fredrickson, B (2011) *Positivity*. London: Oneworld.

Fredrickson, B (2013) Updated Thinking on Positivity Ratios. *American Psychologist*, 68(9): 814–22. doi: 10.1037/a0033584.

Fredrickson, B and Joiner, T (2018) Reflections on Positive Emotions and Upward Spirals. *Perspectives on Psychological Science*, 13(2): 194–9.

Granovetter, M S (1973) The Strength of Weak Ties. *American Journal of Sociology*, 78(6): 1360–80.

Haase, V, Spychalska, M and Werning, M (2019) Investigating the Comprehension of Negated Sentences Employing World Knowledge: An Event-Related Potential Study. *Frontiers in Psychology*, 10. doi: 10.3389/fpsyg.2019.02184.

Health and Safety Executive (2022) Work-related Stress, Anxiety or Depression Statistics in Great Britain 2022. [online] Available at: www.hse.gov.uk/statistics/overall/hssh2122.pdf (accessed 6 March 2023).

Isen, A M, Daubman, K A and Nowicki, G P (1987) Positive Affect Facilitates Creative Problem Solving. *Journal of Personality and Social Psychology*, 52(6): 1122–31.

Kashdan, T and Biswas-Diener, R (2015) *The Upside of Your Dark Side: Why Being Your Whole Self – Not Just Your Good Self – Drives Success and Fulfillment*. New York: Plume Books.

Lomas, T (2016) Towards a Positive Cross-cultural Lexicography: Enriching our Emotional Landscape through 216 'Untranslatable' Words Pertaining to Well-being. *The Journal of Positive Psychology*, 11(5): 546–58.

Losada, M (1999) The Complex Dynamics of High Performance Teams. *Mathematical and Computer Modelling*, 30(9–10): 179–92.

Murray, N, Sujan, H, Hirt, ER and Sujan, M (1990) The Influence of Mood on Categorization: A Cognitive Flexibility Interpretation. *Journal of Personality and Social Psychology*, 59(3): 411–25. doi: 10.1037/0022-3514.59.3.411.

Newberg, A and Waldman, A R (2012) *Words Can Change Your Brain*. New York: Penguin Group.

Ong, A D, Bergemen, C S, Bisconti, T L and Wallace, K A (2006) Psychological Resilience, Positive Emotions, and Successful Adaptation to Stress in Later Life. *Journal of Personality and Social Psychology*, 91(4): 730–49.

Pfeffer, J and Williams, L (2020) Mental Health in the Workplace: The Coming Revolution. *McKinsey Quarterly*. [online] Available at: www.mckinsey.com/industries/healthcare-systems-and-services/our-insights/mental-health-in-the-workplace-the-coming-revolution (accessed 6 March 2023).

Ren, F and Zhang, J (2015) Job Stressors, Organizational Innovation Climate, and Employees' Innovative Behavior. *Creativity Research Journal*, 27(1): 16–23. doi: 10.1080/10400419.2015.992659.

Rowe, G, Hirsh, J B and Anderson, A K (2007) Positive Affect Increases the Breadth of Attentional Selection. *Proceedings of the National Academy of Scientists of the United States of America*, 104(1): 383–8.

Seligman, M E P (2002) *Flourish*. London: Nicholas Brealey Publishing.

Tooby, J and Cosmides, L (2000) The Evolutionary Psychology and the Emotions and Their Relationship to Internal Regulatory Variables. In Lewis, M, Haviland-Jones, J M and Barrett, L F (eds) *Handbook of Emotions* (pp 114–37). London: The Guilford Press.

Wadlinger, H A and Isaacowitz, D M (2006) Positive Mood Broadens Visual Attention to Positive Stimuli. *Motivation and Emotion*, 30(1): 87–99. doi: 10.1007/s11031-006-9021-1.

Woolley, K and Fishbach, A (2016) For the Fun of It: Harnessing Immediate Rewards to Increase Persistence in Long-term Goals. *Journal of Consumer Research*, 42(6): 952–66. .

World Economic Forum (2020) The Future of Jobs Report. [online] Available at: www.weforum.org/reports/the-future-of-jobs-report-2020 (accessed 6 March 2023).

3 Superpowers

In normal life, we keep interrupting what we do with doubts and questions. 'Why am I doing this?' 'Should I perhaps be doing something else?' Repeatedly we question the necessity of our actions and evaluate critically the reasons for carrying them out. But in flow, there is no need to reflect, because the action carries us forward as if by magic.

(Csikszentmihalyi, 2002)

This chapter explores the power of engagement, the E of PERMA and how the more engaged you are with your work and your life, the better you feel, and the more success you have. Being engaged in tasks moment to moment and being engaged and excited by the future both enable well-being and performance.

What does it mean to '*be engaged*' at work?' Being engaged at work is the level of enthusiasm and commitment people have for their jobs. Engaged people will have an emotional and rational attachment to their work and the people they work with. They will also feel an attachment to the goals and vision of the organisation. With this definition, you can see that it is no accident that people refer to the commitment of getting married as '*being engaged*' – that, too, is an emotional attachment to the person they are marrying, with a promise of commitment.

Companies have measured employee engagement for over 30 years, and surveys have shown that employee engagement is strongly linked to the financial performance of the organisation (Smith, 2022). A Gallup Report (the world leader on people data within businesses) found that low employee engagement negatively impacts productivity and profitability. The analysis looked at employee engagement in 192 organisations in 49 industries in 34 countries. They found that employee engagement was related to all nine of the performance outcomes that they studied. When they compared the top quartile of businesses with high engagement versus the bottom quartile, they found that there was a 22 per cent difference in profitability and 21 per cent in productivity (Harter et al, 2013).

We therefore want to increase engagement at work to enable well-being and individual and company performance.

ENGAGEMENT: FLOW

A particular form of engagement that comes from the positive psychology field is flow. Flow is a state of engagement in which you feel energy, enjoyment and focus. I think it is such a lovely word, as it reminds me of the flow of water along a river, moving over obstacles and round bends. The river water moves inexorably and intuitively, but not without effort. The beauty of flow is that, while it feels effortless and enjoyable, it usually requires great mental or physical effort and discipline.

I had planned my day – I would be stopping for a run at 12pm, then after lunch back to the desk at 1:30pm. We measure time in Chronos time (clock time); discrete pieces of time within which to get things done. I had 15 minutes to finish a piece of work, 1 hour and 15 minutes to have lunch and run, then back to the desk to a coaching session. My Chronos clock was well planned and logical.

But something happened, I lost track of time. I became completely engaged in trying to solve something that had been puzzling me with regard to my work. I was so engaged I did not notice the passing of time. I did not check the time, nor my emails or messages. Not until I had understood what had previously been a mystery to me did I then check the time. With a jolt I realised I had 20 minutes for lunch before my next coaching session. I had been fully 'in flow', not aware of what was happening, and not caring about the passing minutes. The challenge had been enough to keep me interested, but not too difficult that I gave up and preferred to run. During that time of flow my engagement in my work was so high that I forgot time.

The Greeks had two different words for the concept of time. They had the concept of Chronos time as we do: the qualitative measurement of time by minutes, hours, weeks, months and years. They also had the concept of Kairos time. Kairos time is entirely different to Chronos time as it is not based on clocks, it is a qualitative measure. In ancient Greek, Kairos means 'right, or opportune moment'. Kairos time is a moment of time in which we make meaning and are unaware of clock time, we are fully engaged in and are enjoying the moment (Chapman, 2014). During that time my work had such meaning that I was fully immersed within it. I was in flow.

Being in flow is a peak state of engagement, which increases a feeling of wellness. Csikszentmihalyi, a psychologist, who first studied and proposed the idea of flow in 1990, said,

> When people were in flow, either at home or in leisure, they reported it as a much more positive experience than the times they were not in flow. When challenges and skills were both high they felt happier, more cheerful, stronger, more active, they concentrated more, they felt more creative and satisfied.
>
> (Csikszentmihalyi, 2002)

Flow is not just about 'not being aware of the clock', it also about not listening to the internal dialogue inside your own head. Do you have a voice in your head that questions you? Sometimes criticises you? Or a voice that commentates for you? Especially when events are not going as well as you would like them to? Many clients I work with hear this voice.

Indeed, it is often this voice that is so destructive to self-confidence and self-esteem and keeps people stuck. There are different psychological models that explain our ability to experience different voices or feel like different people inside our own heads. From the coaching world, Timothy Gallwey, considered one of the founders of coaching, refers to the narrating voice as '*Self 1*'. Self 1 is the critical, commentating voice, interfering with performance and engagement. The other self, '*Self 2*' is the '*doer*', the part of you that does the work. When we are in flow Self 1 is quiet. Gallwey explains that Maslow, a well-known humanistic psychologist, called these flow moments '*peak experiences*'. '*During such experiences, the mind does not act like a separate entity telling you what you should do or criticising how you do it. It is quiet; you are "together", and the action flows as free as a river*' (Gallwey, 1975).

When we are in flow, having a peak experience or '*in the zone*', the voice in our head is quiet. This removes self-doubt, indecision, fear, worries and frustrations. This means much greater performance and enjoyment.

> *... every flow activity, whether it involved competition, chance, or any other dimension of experience, had this in common: It provided a sense of discovery, a creative feeling of transporting the person into a new reality. It pushed the person to higher levels of performance, and led to previously undreamed of states of consciousness.*
>
> (Csikszentmihalyi, 2002)

STRENGTHS, FLOW AND ENGAGEMENT

Knowing about flow is useful and powerful, but it is a bit like knowing how useful and powerful good sleep is. When we sleep well we are rested, energised and more positive. Yet, the worst advice to give someone trying to fall asleep when their Self 1 voice won't be quiet is to say, '*Focus on falling asleep, try hard, think about how great you will feel after a good sleep*'. The act of thinking about falling asleep only causes more anxiety as you are consciously thinking about dropping off. Sleep creeps up on you when you are thinking about something else. When you ensure the conditions for sleep are as good as they can be, then sleep is more likely. Flow is the same. You can't force flow, but you can create the conditions within which flow is more likely to happen.

Csikszentmihalyi said that to foster flow it helps to have these conditions:

- a chance of completing the task;
- the environment for concentration;
- a clear goal;
- a sense of control.

A powerful way to increase your chances of flow and cultivate these conditions is to understand your strengths. When you use your strengths, you are more likely to have a sense of control, a good chance of completing the task and the vision to form a clear goal.

Therefore, using your strengths makes it much more likely that you will experience the peak state of engagement that is flow, and also that you will be more generally engaged in your work by having more enjoyment in it (Wagner et al, 2020).

A Gallup study in 22 organisations across 45 countries found that '*people who use their strengths every day are more than three times more likely to report having an excellent quality of life and six times more likely to be engaged at work*' (Rigoni and Asplund, 2016).

Imagine knowing that whenever you face a challenge you already have something inside of you that is able to help and support you through that time. Something that is easily accessible, readily available, easy to use, familiar and helpful. When you know your strengths you can bring them to challenges, choose roles, projects and assignments that match your strengths, choose to work with people who have complementary strengths and systematically develop the strengths you need to do the role you have.

Your strengths are latent powers that increase your engagement: you can use them to support your well-being and drive your performance with enjoyment. They are unique to you and endlessly powerful. Your strengths can also guide you to know where to put your effort, and what goals to go after. If to attain the goal you need to use your strengths, then you are far more likely to stay motivated. Knowing the strengths of your team can be equally powerful.

Despite their power, many people just don't know or don't appreciate their own strengths. Because negativity can be more '*sticky*', we tend to know our weaknesses and mistakes, and we strive to improve our weaknesses and rectify our shortfallings, above maximising our strengths. Negativity is more sticky as in ancient times being aware of dangers was a matter of survival, so awareness of danger is wired into our genes. Also, psychologists have shown that our brains remember negative events more easily than positive happenings (Jarwoski, 2020). Most people in the corporate world will have a development plan that seeks to address their weaknesses so that they can move on in their careers. Far fewer people in the corporate world will have a plan to maximise strengths. Being aware and then actively using strengths based on that awareness is the key to flourishing. A study of 10,000 workers in New Zealand found that people who were aware of their strengths were 9.5 times more likely to be flourishing, and those that were aware *and* used their strengths were 18 times more likely to be flourishing at work (Hone et al, 2015).

CHARACTER STRENGTHS

Positive psychologists describe different types of strengths. Talents are our innate abilities, such as a talent for music or languages. Skills are proficiencies we learn, such as IT skills or people skills that we have developed through learning and practice. We also have our character strengths. *Character strengths*, a fundamental part of positive psychology, are positive traits that help the fulfilment of yourself or others. Positive psychologists describe character strengths as distinct from talents, skills and interests. Character strengths are what makes you '*you*', and when you use your character strengths you are far more likely to flourish. There is a psychologically validated test developed by positive psychologists called the Values in Action Inventory (VIA) that can be completed to understand your own character strengths. All of the 24 character strengths are on a continuum; it is not the case that you have a strength or don't have it. You just have stronger and lesser strengths.

The survey also tells you your *signature strengths* – your top superpowers. Signature strengths are the strengths that matter most to you; they will be your greatest strengths and will often be so much part of your identity that you would struggle to live without them.

The best way to understand if a strength is really a signature strength is to imagine living without it for a week and reflecting how you would find it. One of my signature strengths is hope. If I had to live for one day without any hope it seems impossible, and you will feel the same for your signature strengths.

The 24 character strengths in the survey are classified under six virtues. The strengths classification has been translated into 40 languages and 7 million people have completed it from 195 countries (every country in the world). If you are interested to find out more about the survey and take the survey yourself, you can visit www.viacharacter.org/.

Included here are all character strengths, classified under the six virtues (www.viacharacter. org/character-strengths).

- **Wisdom – learning and gathering knowledge**
  Creativity: original; adaptive; ingenuity
  Curiosity: interest; novelty-seeking; exploration; openness to experience
  Judgement: critical thinking; thinking things through; open-minded
  Love of learning: mastering new skills and topics; systematically adding to knowledge
  Perspective: wisdom; providing wise counsel; taking the big picture view

- **Courage – tackling adversity**
  Bravery: valour; not shrinking from fear; speaking up for what's right
  Perseverance: persistence; industry; finishing what one starts
  Honesty: authenticity; integrity
  Zest: vitality; enthusiasm; vigour; energy; feeling alive and activated

- **Humanity – building and maintaining positive relationships with others**
  Love: both loving and being loved; valuing close relations with others
  Kindness: generosity; nurturance; care; compassion; altruism; '*niceness*'
  Social intelligence: aware of the motives/feelings of oneself and others

- **Justice – relating to those around us**
  Teamwork: citizenship; social responsibility; loyalty
  Fairness: just; not letting feelings bias decisions about others
  Leadership: organising group activities; encouraging a group to get things done

- **Temperance – managing habits and protecting against excess**
  Forgiveness: mercy; accepting others' shortcomings; giving people a second chance
  Humility: modesty; letting one's accomplishments speak for themselves
  Prudence: careful; cautious; not taking undue risks
  Self-regulation: self-control; disciplined; managing impulses and emotions

- **Transcendence – connecting in a meaningful way to the world around us**
  Appreciation of beauty and excellence: awe; wonder; elevation
  Gratitude: thankful for the good; expressing thanks; feeling blessed
  Hope: optimism; future-mindedness; future orientation
  Humour: playfulness; bringing smiles to others
  Spirituality: religiousness; faith; purpose; meaning

There are other strengths questionnaires available; a well-known one is the Gallup CliftonStrengths finder that includes strengths in strategic thinking, relationships building, influencing, and executing. You can find this strengths finder at: www.gallup.com/clifton strengths/en/252137/home.aspx.

You can of course also reflect on your own strengths without the use of a questionnaire by asking yourself the following questions.

- What do you love doing?
- What are you naturally good at?
- What positive feedback do you usually get from others?
- What positive words do you think define you?

You can also seek feedback from others on what strengths they see in you.

When I ask my clients about their strengths, I often find that people are far more comfortable talking about their weaknesses; often they won't have stopped to consider where their strengths lie, how they use them or what other people perceive their strengths to be. They also won't necessarily have thought about developing their strengths further. In sports coaching it is common to take a strength and make it a super strength, such as a strong serve in tennis becoming a defining strength of a player's game that gets better and better with practice. Yet in the business world it is far less common to take that approach. Strengths may be recognised, but they are far less commonly focused on as a development area. Managers may think, '*Why develop a strength? Let's focus on weaknesses instead, then we will have well rounded team member.*'

Not maximising strengths or not developing strengths means you are underutilising one of the key ways you can drive your own performance at work, and the performance of others, and a key way that you and your teams can stay motivated, happy and well through more flow and higher engagement. Seligman says, '*We can all be winners when acting in accordance with strengths and virtues*' (Seligman, 2002).

STRENGTHS TO IMPROVE PERFORMANCE AND WELL-BEING

Increasing the use of strengths at work has been shown in numerous studies to improve performance at work. A key workplace study found that the use of signature strengths at work is a crucial predictor of workplace outcomes. The more you can use your signature strengths, the more successful you are at work. The same study also found that creativity and teamwork were two signature strengths that strongly correlated with high workplace outcomes (Harter et al, 2013). Knowing your own strengths and using your signature strengths also helps you to achieve your goals (Linley et al, 2010).

A study of nearly 2000 workers investigated what happened when sales staff received strengths coaching compared to those who had no strengths coaching. Those who received the coaching had higher productivity rates (Asplund and Blacksmith, 2011). A second study with over 65,000 people showed that employees who had feedback on their strengths were far more likely to stay with their organisations; turnover rates were nearly 15 per cent lower for those who had received the feedback (Asplund and Blacksmith, 2011).

Using your strengths day-to-day also strongly improves well-being. '*The more hours a day adults believe they use their strengths, the more likely they are to report having ample energy, feeling well-rested, being happy, smiling or laughing a lot, learning something interesting, and being treated with respect*' (Rigoni and Asplund, 2016).

There are also particular character strengths that are strongly associated with well-being. People who have these as character strengths are far more likely to say they have good well-being.

Table 3.1 Character strengths strongly associated with well-being

Zest	Connects you happily to the here and now
Curiosity	
Love	Connects you to a life of fulfilment
Hope	Connects you happily to the future
Gratitude	Connects you happily to the past

There are also character strengths that are most strongly associated with workplace well-being: zest, teamwork, hope, love, gratitude, leadership, and perseverance (Harzer et al, 2017).

OVERUSE OF STRENGTHS

Using our strengths is motivational and powerful, but we do need to be mindful of overusing or overplaying particular strengths. If we overuse a strength then we can become tired of it, just like an athlete who may use the same muscles over and over again and needs to rest their muscles before training or competing again. It is important to rest our strengths so that their use does not become toxic to ourselves or others. You may also overuse a strength because it is comfortable. Over-relying on a particular strength can happen out of habit. Overplaying a strength can also crowd out other strengths, like a dominant plant crowding out the light of other growing greenery, or our strengths can become our comfort zone where we stay to shield ourselves from change or challenge. Often at some point in the journey to the C-suite, leaders realise the strengths that they have which got them so far won't necessarily ensure that they can reach the next level. They now need to develop their lesser strengths to meet their next challenges.

So, how do we know when a strength is being overused?

I have recently coached a senior leader who has a strength of being incredibly delivery focused. His colleagues know that his team will deliver what the organisation needs because he has a great ability to drive himself and his team to meet tight deadlines with quality work. However, when this strength is overplayed he can focus so much on getting work over the line that the motivation of his team can struggle. How does he know he is overplaying his strength? Feedback. Feedback is a powerful mirror that we need to look into regularly and with curiosity to hear what is working and what is not working. An overplayed strength is often in our blind spot, something we are not aware of because we are enjoying using the strength and it feels natural to us. We need the calibration of others to help us see if a super strength has actually become a lesser strength because it is crowding out all other strengths.

Overplaying a strength can also lead you to enjoy using that strength less. For example, I coached someone who had a signature strength of perseverance. They were the person who would not give up, who always wanted to see a project through to the end despite any difficulties. But this was being overplayed due to relentless amounts of work the person had to get through. As they felt that being perseverant defined them, it was part of them, then stepping back to look after their own energy levels and well-being felt impossible before coaching. Through coaching we explored how perseverance is a behaviour, and behaviours can be changed, and how they could use their strength of perseverance in a new way – to persevere with looking after themselves as well as persevering with their work. The overplayed strength could be harnessed to help solve the situation.

To help you manage your strengths and not overplay them, it is worthwhile doing an exercise on your top strengths (either those from the VIA categories, or from another strengths-based finder, or through your own reflections). You can list your top five strengths and then ask yourself the following questions.

- What does it look like if I overplay strength X?
- What will I see?
- What will I feel?
- Who would know that I am overplaying that strength, and how will they know?

By asking these questions pre-emptively, you will know what warning signs or trigger signs to look for when a strength is being overplayed.

INTRINSIC MOTIVATION

Strengths help encourage flow and engagement because using strengths means we tap into a certain type of motivation. Motivation is having a reason that gives us energy to do something. Without that reason we may *want* to act, but struggle to find the energy to do so. The reason to act can either be an intrinsic reason, or extrinsic.

Intrinsic motivation means the reason we act is because doing the action will satisfy our basic needs to live in line with our values, do things we enjoy, connect with others and contribute to our workplaces/communities/families/friendships.

When we are intrinsically motivated to do something it is when we are using our strengths to do something we enjoy just for the enjoyment of doing it. Intrinsic motivators include challenging work, growth and learning. Extrinsic motivators mean the reason we act is to gain something outside of ourselves such as more money, recognition or a promotion, or to avoid punishment. The psychologist Frederick Herzberg introduced the idea of hygiene factors (extrinsic motivators) and motivation factors (intrinsic motivators). His theory is called the Two Factor Theory, introduced in a famous article called *One More Time: How Do You Motivate Employees?* (Herzberg, 2003). He says: '*The surest way of getting someone to do something is to deliver a kick in the pants – put bluntly, the KITA … But while a KITA might produce some change in behaviour, it doesn't motivate.*' He goes on to explain that intrinsic factors, which he calls an internal generator, are what motivates people. Herzberg proposed that intrinsic and extrinsic motivators have an inverse relationship. This means intrinsic motivators increase motivation when they are present; conversely, extrinsic motivators reduce motivation when they are absent.

We can have goals that are inherently intrinsic – they are goals to gain achievements, have growth or overcome challenges. We can also have extrinsic goals such as salary or wealth. We can have a balance of intrinsic and extrinsic goals in our lives and careers. If we just have extrinsic goals then we are more likely to suffer stress, burn-out, and feel anxious and lonely. We can end up having a crisis of meaning – *'Why am I here and what is it all for?'*. If we just have intrinsic goals then we can end up having a crisis of duality, where we can feel we have not achieved what we want to achieve in life, such as a certain level of wealth, or career progress. When a goal is intrinsic it has been shown to lead to better performance, better interpersonal relationships and a greater ability to adapt and therefore respond to change (Zhang et al, 2018).

Table 3.2 Intrinsic and extrinsic motivation

Intrinsic motivation	Extrinsic motivation
Satisfy our basic needs based on our core interests, passions and values. For example, personal growth, positive relationships, physical health, contribution.	Satisfy our need for external rewards or the positive recognition of others. For example, wealth, fame, power, promotion.

Using strengths in day-to-day life helps you to feel intrinsically motivated by the things you are doing and therefore more engaged because naturally you enjoy what you are doing, and you have innate satisfaction from what you are doing, which means you are motivated to do it, without worrying about the external results.

GROWING ENGAGEMENT IN THE WORKPLACE

We will now look at some practical tools and techniques that can increase engagement at work by using strengths, increasing intrinsic motivation and increasing the chances of flow.

Tapping into strengths

To be able to tap into the power of strengths to increase the likelihood of flow, and increase engagement, the first step is to know and understand your individual strengths. In their book on strengths and leadership, Rath and Conchie (2009) say:

> If you spend your life trying to be good at everything, you will never be great at anything. While our society encourages us to be well rounded, this approach inadvertently breeds mediocrity. Perhaps the greatest misconception of all is the well-rounded leader. Without an awareness of your strengths it's almost impossible for you to lead effectively. We all lead in very different ways based on our talents and limitations.

While their work focuses on leaders, this theory applies to everyone; without an awareness of our strengths it is impossible for us to fulfil our potential. Therefore, the first step in using strengths to help with engagement is to be sure of what your strengths are. There are a number of ways to do this. You could reflect on your own strengths by listing:

- five things you are good at;
- five positive words to describe yourself;
- five skills you have learnt during your career;
- five things you enjoy doing.

Combine this with asking colleagues and friends to tell you three strengths they see in you.

INDIVIDUAL PPI

You can take the free VIA survey at www.viacharacter.org/survey/account/Register and find out your character strengths.

The survey will give you the full list of character strengths in order of strongest to lesser strengths. This exercise is a further exploration of strengths.

Once you have your results, ask yourself these questions.

- What are my signature strengths? (Top five)
- When have I used my signature strengths in the last week and how did they help me?
- Which signature strength could I make more use of?
- Which lesser strengths do I most need to develop?
- How could I use my signature strengths in new ways at work or home?

Strengths in teams

Knowing your own strengths is powerful, and knowing others' strengths, such as those of colleagues and team members, is equally powerful. When you know your team members' strengths you can help them to have more flow in their work, and you have a lever for increasing their intrinsic motivation and therefore their engagement. Having a team strengths session is an excellent way to increase engagement.

You can brainstorm and discuss as a team:

- common strengths;
- unique strengths;
- matched strengths;
- underused strengths;
- overused strengths;
- visible strengths;
- invisible strengths;
- complementary strengths.

You can then use this sharing of knowledge to plan how you can maximise the use of strengths in the team. You can also ensure that you show gratitude for people's strengths by giving supportive feedback: '*You were so creative in the team meeting, I loved hearing all of your thoughts, it really helped us as a team to see things differently.*' Or you can savour any successes that have happened because of team strengths – celebrate and congratulate these in team meetings for achievements.

TEAM PPI

Strengths spotting

Put the team into pairs and allow ten minutes per round.

Each person has to guess the top three strengths of the other person (using the VIA character strengths list), taking it in turns to ask these questions and also basing their guess on what they have seen in the workplace.

- What is an ideal work day for you?
- What activities give you energy at work?
- What activities at work would you most miss if you couldn't do them?
- When do you become completely absorbed at work and lose track of time?
- What are you most proud of in your career?

When they have decided what the top three might be, they then give feedback to say when they have seen that strength in action at work.

This works as a great feel-good exercise as people receive positive feedback while also then sharing their actual top three strengths. It can provoke a discussion on what strengths are visible at work and why, and whether you could actively use a strength more. It also helps develop people to start spotting strengths.

Appreciative inquiry (AI)

AI is an approach that is used in the workplace that focuses on strengths and a positive approach to leadership and organisational change. It has been used effectively in many private and public sector organisations to enable positive change. AI was originally developed by David Cooperrider in the US to help organisations transform. The Positive Psychology movement adopted it as a tool for personal development.

AI is based on the idea that people and organisations '*shift*', they are not '*fixed*' – they are not problems to be solved. AI is based on five principles:

1. the constructivist principle – what we pay attention to grows;
2. the simultaneity principle – how inquiry (questioning) helps change to occur;
3. the anticipatory principle – how powerful it is to have a vision, as we can anticipate the future;

4. the positive principle – our positive emotions build our capacity;
5. the poetic principle – we have the power to pivot and choose a different direction.

AI has four stages. The first is the Discovery phase, which is all about hunting for the good. The participants involved in the initiative using AI (for example, the project team) first explore the organisation's (or team's, or individual's) strengths, what are the best practices in the organisation, when has the organisation been at peak performance and what enabled that. The next stage is called Dream, where the team agree a future they would like – a vision – that is based on the idea of people in the organisation being fully engaged in the purpose of the organisation. The third is Design, which is the designing of strategies to move the organisation towards that vision. The last is Destiny, when the strategies are executed and revised as needed.

AI is possibly the most well-known and established positive intervention that is used in the workplace and there are books dedicated to applying AI in organisations (Cooperrider and Whitney, 2005). AI has extremely close links with the E of PERMA, and indeed with the other letters of PERMA too. As we have talked about in this chapter, focusing on strengths and what is best can help drive positive change, and that is the essence of AI.

Enabling intrinsic motivation

Using strengths helps us to be intrinsically motivated. There are also other practical ways we can help others to tap into their intrinsic motivations. Deci and Ryan, two psychologists who met in 1977 and have worked together for decades later, revolutionised the way we view motivation through their Self-Determination Theory. An early experiment in forming their theory involved asking two groups of students to solve cube puzzles in two different rooms. In one room the group were paid for each puzzle they solved. In the other there was no payment. Both groups were asked to return, and once again they were put into two rooms and asked to solve puzzles. During the experiment, the groups were left alone in the rooms for a short time. The group that had been paid the first time tended to stop solving the puzzles and they also solved them less well. In the group that had not been paid students tended to continue to solve the puzzles and their performance was better than the other group. Deci and Ryan concluded that offering a reward to the first group had reduced their intrinsic motivation. The second group still had intrinsic motivation from the enjoyment of solving the puzzles and sense of accomplishment. Deci and Ryan found that certain actions increase intrinsic motivation: giving freedom of choice, feeling confident, receiving positive feedback and acknowledging emotions.

Their theory describes that we all have three basic needs that need to be met for us to feel intrinsically motivated. The first is *autonomy*. We need to feel that we have an element of choice in what we do and how we do it, so that we do not feel restricted or trapped. The second is *relatedness*. We want to feel connected to others and that we belong to something. The third is *competence* – we want to feel that we are effective at something. When these basic needs are met then we are much more likely to feel motivated. You can help meet these basic needs for others by your own behaviour as a manager or leader or colleague (Deci and Ryan, 2012).

Table 3.3 Basic needs and behaviours to meet these needs

Basic need	Behaviour to create conditions for basic needs to be met
Autonomy	Empowering others
Relatedness	Bringing people together Shared goals Shared successes
Competence	Giving positive feedback to others

SUMMARY CHECKLIST

To increase engagement and flow at work for yourself and others:

- uncover your key strengths;
- share your strengths with your team;
- bring your strengths to challenges;
- use your strengths in new ways;
- beware of overusing or just relying on key strengths.

Find out the strengths of your colleagues and team and notice and give positive feedback to people when you see them using their strengths.

Enable intrinsic motivation by meeting the three basic conditions of being motivated: autonomy, relatedness and competence.

REFLECTIONS

What is so liberating about truly understanding strengths is the realisation that particular strengths are not something that we have or do not have, all strengths are on a continuum. Our weaknesses are our lesser strengths. Some strengths can show up strongly at work, but disappear altogether at home. Ryan Niemic, who has done much of the recent leading research on strengths, emphasises the power of using strengths in new ways. We can get into habits where we only use them in certain situations, when triggered to use them. For example, the excellent manager who has endless patience in a 1:1 to develop a team member, who is then impatient and distracted at home because they are thinking about work (and the development of their team!).

I'm often asked by clients: can your signature strengths change over time? And the answer is yes, of course they can – through concerted effort because you want them to, or because a life change has happened, and you change as a result. I first did the VIA survey four years ago and found my five signature strengths. When I later did the survey again at the end of 2020, my signature strengths had changed. I found that zest had decreased dramatically from a higher strength to a lesser strength, which was actually quite upsetting for me. During the time that it changed my husband had fallen seriously ill, twice. First he was diagnosed with cancer and had an operation to remove the tumour, then on a family holiday he fell ill with pneumonia and flu, which then developed suddenly and unexpectedly into sepsis. He spent two weeks in intensive care, most of it in an induced coma, and then a further two weeks in hospital. He had a long recovery afterwards back to health. During this time I needed some of my signature strengths more than ever – hope, gratitude (that he was still alive), self-regulation and perseverance. But zest – approaching life with excitement and energy; not doing things halfway or half-heartedly; living life as an adventure; feeling alive and activated – was not a priority. I visited intensive care with quiet calmness and love but not with a sense of adventure or excitement.

As he returned to health and I then had the long lockdown, home schooling four children, I struggled to rekindle the sense of adventure and feeling fully alive. My signature strength of self-regulation became a key part of managing the day – timetables and routines. As the world is returning to normal, and my husband is having a stable period of good health, I have been actively looking to develop what was then a lesser strength – zest. I re-did the survey again in April 2022 and zest has moved back up the list to one of my signature strengths through me actively focusing and being aware that it is a strength I want to be defined by and that I find helps me in my work and life. Many of my clients feel freed by the thought that they can choose to develop a signature strength or a lesser strength, and this feeds into our basic needs for motivation – we can have an element of control over what we are good at.

SELF-COACHING QUESTIONS

Work through GROW for this topic and do add more questions/reflections at each stage than are detailed here if you want to explore further.

Goal (to uncover what your aim is)

- What specifically would I like to improve with regard to:
  - my engagement at work?
  - my team's engagement?
  - my organisation's engagement? (for business owners and senior leadership teams)

Reality (to understand)

- What is going on for me that makes this something I would like to change?
- What is going on for my team that makes this something I would like to change?
- If my team was exceptionally engaged, what would we be doing differently?
- If I was exceptionally engaged at work, what would I be doing differently?

Options (to explore)

- What could I do to increase engagement at work for myself and for my team?
- How could I use my strengths more at work?
- How can I understand the strengths of my team more?

Will (to decide on action)

- What do I need to do now?
- What is the first step I will take and when?
- What deadlines will I set for myself?

REFERENCES

Asplund, J and Blacksmith, N (2011) How Strengths Boost Engagement. *Gallup Business Journal.* [online] Available at: https://static1.squarespace.com/static/578c4a19197aea41c7eed064/t/59af9b4cf9a61eccbf96cb5f/1504680785048/How+Strengths+Boost+Engagement.pdf (accessed 6 March 2023).

Chapman, S (2014) *Can Scorpians Smoke?* London: Change and Creativity.

Cooperrider, D and Whitney, D (2005) *Appreciative Inquiry: A Positive Revolution in Change.* London: Berrett-Koehler.

Csikszentmihalyi, M (2002) *Flow.* New York: Harper and Row.

Deci, E L and Ryan, R M (2012) Self-determination Theory. In Van Lange, P A M, Kruglanski, A W and Higgins, E T (eds) *Handbook of Theories of Social Psychology* (pp 416–37). Thousand Oaks, CA: Sage.

Gallwey, T W (1975) *The Inner Game of Tennis.* London: Jonathan Cape.

Harter, J K et al (2013) *The Relationship between Engagement at Work and Organisational Outcomes 2012 Meta-analysis.* Gallup Inc. [online] Available at: https://employeeengagement.com/wp-content/uploads/2013/04/2012-Q12-Meta-Analysis-Research-Paper.pdf (accessed 6 March 2023).

Harzer, C, Mubashar, T and Dubreuil, P (2017) Character Strengths and Strength-related Person-job Fit as Predictors of Work-related wellbeing, Job Performance, and Workplace Deviance. *Wirtschaftspsychologie,* 19(3): 23–38.

Herzberg, F (2003) One More Time: How do You Motivate Employees? *Harvard Business Review,* 81: 87–96. doi: 10.1007/978-1-349-02701-9_2.

Hone, L C, Jarden, A, Duncan, S and Schofield, G M (2015) Flourishing in New Zealand Workers: Associations with Lifestyle Behaviors, Physical Health, Psychosocial, and Work-related Indicators. *Journal of Occupational and Environmental Medicine,* 57(9): 973–83.

Jarwoski, M (2020) The Negativity Bias: Why the Bad Stuff Sticks. Psycom. [online] Available at: www.psycom.net/negativity-bias (accessed 6 March 2023).

Linley, P A, Nielsen, K, Wood, A M, Gillett, R and Biswas-Diener, R (2010) Using Signature Strengths in Pursuit of Goals: Effects on Goal Progress, Need Satisfaction, and Well-being, and Implications for Coaching Psychologists. *International Coaching Psychology Review,* 5(1): 6–15.

Rath, T and Conchie, B (2009) *Strengths Based Leadership: Great Leaders, Teams, and Why People Follow.* New York: Gallup Press.

Rigoni, B and Asplund, J (2016) Developing Employees Strengths Boosts Sales Profits and Engagement. *Harvard Business Review.* [online] Available at: https://hbr.org/2016/09/developing-employees-strengths-boosts-sales-profit-and-engagement (accessed 7 March 2023).

Seligman, M E P (2002) *Authentic Happiness.* London: Nicholas Brealey Publishing.

Smith, T (2022) What is Employee Engagement? Investopedia. [online] Available at: www.investopedia.com/terms/e/employee-engagement.asp (accessed 7 March 2023).

Wagner, L, Holenstein, M, Wepf, H and Ruch, W (2020) Character Strengths are Related to Students' Achievement, Flow Experiences, and Enjoyment in Teacher-centered Learning, Individual, and Group Work Beyond Cognitive Ability. *Frontiers in Psychology*, 11. doi: 10.3389/fpsyg.2020.01324.

Zhang, Y, Zhang, J and Li, J (2018) The Effect of Intrinsic and Extrinsic Goals on Work Performance: Prospective and Empirical Studies on Goal Content Theory. *Personnel Review*, 47(4): 900–12. doi: 10.1108/PR-03-2017-0086.

4

People matter

... Happiness happens with others ... If selfish happiness is the only goal of your life, your life will soon be goal-less.

(Ricard, 2018)

This chapter explores the power of relationships, the R of PERMA, and how the more positive and supportive your relationships are at work, the better your performance and your feelings of well-being.

Does happiness exist inside of you in isolation of and despite others? Self-help books sometimes encourage this idea – that you can read a book and find happiness and fulfilment within yourself despite circumstances and other people. Certainly, many ideas in this book can be carried out on your own and support you in managing your thoughts and feelings to enhance your well-being and positivity at work. But working on yourself in a vacuum is like trying to lead a revolution on your own, without supporters, followers, cheerleaders or motivators.

Happiness is not just inside people, it is between people, within communities, and built into cultures, friendships and families. Harnessing the power of positivity and happiness cannot be a lonely mission. Happiness is not *just* a state that sits inside someone, still and empowering, but it is also a thread of contagious energy that exists between people and within communities and workplaces. Positive relationships help us thrive at work, positive leaders help their teams thrive and positive businesses help communities thrive. In this chapter we will look at how positive relationships have a profound impact on well-being and performance and explore practical ideas of how to develop positive relationships at work.

'*In the context of co-responsibility happiness is not a self-help pursuit, but rather a collective enterprise*' (Ahuvia et al, 2015).

THE POTENCY OF POSITIVE RELATIONSHIPS

Chris Peterson, a psychologist and colleague of Martin Seligman even went as far as saying that you can sum up positive psychology in one sentence – '*Other people matter*' (Peterson, 2008). This shows the profound importance of others in positive psychology interventions. Humans are social beings. What we will discuss in this chapter is crucial when considering remote and hybrid working patterns which mean people have fewer opportunities for incidental social interactions. Social support increases the chances of having a long healthy life more than not smoking, not being obese or the level of alcohol consumed (Mertika et al, 2020). Numerous recent studies have shown that supportive relationships mean less chance of illness and greater mental well-being. A study in 2009 showed that your chance of feeling happy is increased by 15 per cent if you have a happy friend (Christakis and Fowler, 2009).

When I first started my career as a graduate trainee at a pharmaceutical company, I spent time moving into different departments to understand the manufacturing process, and build my professional network across the manufacturing site. In one of my work placements I attended the daily leadership planning meeting for the manufacturing lines. These meetings were the first time I became really interested in *how* people get things done at work through their interpersonal skills and relationships (rather than just what people *do* to get things done). The team manager whom I was working for in the placement asked me to observe the communication between all the different characters in the room and reflect on where the power was. Who influenced whom? Who motivated whom? Who demotivated whom? The team manager also gave me a book on leadership that is still a favourite of mine to this day – *Zapp!* by William Byham and Jeff Cox. The book is a fictional tale of managers (including a key character called Joe) in a workplace who either Zapp their teams, which means to energise and motivate, or Sapp their teams, which means to de-energise and demotivate, through the way they communicate with their team members (Byham and Cox, 1991). The idea of a bolt of energy passing between two people when there is positive communication has really stuck with me throughout my career.

The book explores Joe's journey as he finds out more about how to Zapp and how not to Sapp. He makes a list of examples that Sapp energy at work: confusion, lack of trust, not being listened to, no time to solve problems, office politics, no time to work on bigger issues, not knowing whether you are succeeding, across the board rules and regulations, a boss taking credit for another's ideas, not enough resources to do the job, believing that you can't make a difference, a job simplified to the point that it has no meaning, and people treated exactly the same, like interchangeable parts. Joe discovers that there are some key behaviours he can show that will help him Zapp others: maintain self-esteem; listen and respond with empathy; ask for help in solving problems; and offer help without taking responsibility. The importance of this book in regard to positive energy is that Zapping can only happen between two or more people. It is the communication between the two people that creates the Zapp, and therefore motivates and engages all those involved in the interaction – the power of positive communication.

There are two theories as to why positive social interactions help us. The first is called the 'Stress Buffering Hypothesis'; this theory says that we are all likely to experience stressful events in our lives, and if we have positive relationships then we can deal with the stressful events far better than we could if we just had negative relationships, or we dealt with them on our own (Cohen and Wills, 1985). The second theory is called the 'Main Effects Model'. This theory says that having positive social relationships encourages people to build healthier habits, and that people experience a sense of belonging which is critical to well-being. Importantly, both theories are grounded in positive relationships leading to improved well-being. It is this link that summarises nicely why relationships are important at work – they support well-being (Cohen and Wills, 1985).

When we have positive interactions with others our bodies respond physiologically to the interaction. As we looked at in the chapter on positive emotions, we feel positive emotions and these help our minds and bodies to manage stress and find meaning. An example of this is the reduced cortisol circulating in our bodies when we have a positive interaction with someone else. We will also have the release of oxytocin, a happy hormone that helps us feel more motivated and social.

The relationships people have with their colleagues at work is critical to well-being and also performance. Work relationships have been shown to be the most important factor in how engaged employees feel at work (SHRM Report, 2016).

Positive social interactions at work have vast benefits

Table 4.1 Benefits of social interactions at work

Benefit
Facilitate innovative thinking
Increase positive feelings at the end of a work-day
Develop trusting relationships
Increase motivation
Increase job satisfaction
Reduce staff turnover

(Oh et al, 2004; Moynihan and Pandey, 2008; Basford and Offermann, 2012; Wang et al, 2015.)

Barbara Fredrickson, a positive psychologist who has done ground-breaking research in the power of positive emotions, says that we should focus on developing high quality connections. She describes these connections as *'life giving'*. There are four ways to build these connections. The first is being present in conversations you have with others, the second is being supportive of the other person, having the mindset of wanting to help the other person achieve. The third is showing the other person that you are willing to build trust with them, and the fourth is allowing time for non-action/goal-focused communication (Fredrickson, 2011).

Importantly, positive emotions are contagious between people at work. When you are positive you have a major impact on those around you; this is called relational energy. Catching emotions is called emotional contagion. Positive relational energy is energy passed between people that uplifts them and enthuses them.

> Researchers have found that when subjects 'catch' positive emotions from others, they're more likely to be viewed by others and view themselves as more cooperative and competent.
>
> (Bourg Carter, 2012)

To what extent are you a positive energiser in your workplace? To what extent do you infect others with your positivity? Often the most negative people believe that happiness can be found through external circumstances and must be given from other people or particular circumstances. They may start sentences with '*If only X then I would feel much better*'. Or '*When X happens, I will feel Y*'. They believe that responsibility for workplace positive emotions lies outside of them, not within them, or between them and others.

Crucially, negative emotions are just as contagious as positive emotions. How you communicate emotions with others has a direct impact on their emotions. If you are surrounded by people who are acting negatively (a toxic workplace), you will also begin to feel and act negatively. If you act negatively and communicate your thoughts or feelings, then this will be '*caught*' by others around you.

'*During human interactions, people tend to align with the emotional state of the other person, in terms not only of emotionally empathizing with the other but also of mimicking facial expressions and copying bodily changes*' (Herrando and Constantinidis, 2021). We can also see the power of positive relationships at work, just by looking at what happens when we have the opposite. A study that asked people about their negative experiences at work found a multitude of issues that negative relationships cause, including a breakdown in communication, lack of cooperation, stress and decreased motivation (Morrison and Nolan, 2007).

While developing positive relationships and communicating positively are vital elements of developing well-being and performance at work, this does not mean that you should remove yourself from all relationships/people or interactions that are '*negative*'. A black-and-white view of positive/negative interactions or relationships is harmful and limiting as it can lead to judgement of others and yourself, can be isolating and can lead to feelings of being a victim of others' negativity. From my experience working with clients, the people who say they remove all '*negative*' people from their lives are usually very lonely people. No one is a '*negative*' or '*positive*' person. Healthy relationships in and outside of work are usually highs and lows and every shade of grey in between. To really understand the R of PERMA, it is about consciously aiming to develop positive relationships and knowing how to manage interactions or relationships that are not always positive, where there may be pain, anger, disappointment, competitiveness, suspicion or frustration. Being able to manage and be positive in all sorts of interactions, with different people and in different situations, is enormously powerful in helping you to perform well and feel well at work.

EMPATHY AND COMPASSION

There are three key skills that help enable you to build positive relationships at work – empathy, compassion and self-awareness. Empathy is the ability to understand and share the feelings of someone else. When you are able to '*share*' the feelings of another this means being able to appreciate the person's thoughts and feelings from their point of view. There are two powerful benefits of having empathy. The first is that, as neuroscientists have shown, sharing similar emotions to another means we are able to react in a more useful and responsive way to the other person's needs. The second is that empathy enables us to learn about our world. If we see that someone has been hurt by something or a certain situation, then we may develop caution also for that thing or that situation that may serve to protect ourselves (Ricard, 2018). There are different types of empathy.

Table 4.2 Different types of empathy

Types of empathy	Response	Direction of response
Cognitive empathy	Taking the perspective of another Understanding another's situation Understanding another's feelings	Towards self – *'I understand how you feel'*
Emotional/affective empathy	Sharing an emotional response with another Feeling distress in response to someone's pain Feeling joy in response to someone's joy/happiness	Towards self – *'I feel how you feel'*
Somatic empathy	Having a physical reaction in response to what someone else is feeling, eg blushing when someone else is blushing	Towards self – *'I am reacting in the same way as you'*
Compassionate empathy/ empathic concern	Being aware of another's needs and feeling a desire to come to their aid	Towards another – *'I understand how you feel and I want to respond sensitively to your needs'*

Empathy is touted as a key leadership and workplace skill. Indeed, it is a vital skill for leaders as it enables the leader to really understand their team, and subsequently make decisions based on that knowledge. However, it is crucial to appreciate that what we do with our empathy matters; it is not enough just to have it. Empathy can be viewed in two parts. The first is knowing and understanding how another is thinking and feeling. The second is responding with sensitivity to the other. A psychopath can have really developed cognitive empathy, but they can either ignore that knowledge or use it for their own gain, rather than using their empathic skills for the support of others.

The downside of cognitive, emotional and somatic empathy is that they can lead to empathic distress. During the pandemic many healthcare professionals reported feeling empathic distress – *'the strong aversive and self-oriented response to the suffering of others, accompanied by the desire to withdraw from a situation in order to protect one's self from excessive negative feelings'* (Dowling, 2018).

Being subjected to repeated instances of others' suffering can mean we develop empathic distress when we take on the pain of the other person. The ability to distinguish between *'self'* and *'other'* becomes blurred, and we have strong feelings of wanting to protect ourselves as we cannot bear to feel the other person's pain so acutely and the associated negative emotions from that pain. While other workplaces outside of healthcare are not managing life and death situations, empathic distress can still occur in challenging and difficult periods in any workplace.

Therefore, while empathy is useful as it gives us insight and perspective, it should also come with a health warning. Empathy can be damaging to performance and well-being if it leads to empathic distress through repeated use of the skill in a very difficult time.

The second skill that helps us manage relationships through good and difficult times is compassion. Compassion is non-judgemental thinking towards another combined with a feeling of warmth and desire for the others' well-being. Combining empathy and compassion gives us compassionate empathy. I like to think of this as an empathy super-power, with two potent skills mixed together to super charge your relationships and feeling of well-being. Matthieu Ricard – who is often described as the happiest man in the world – started his career as a biochemist and then moved to the Himalayas to become a Buddhist monk. He describes the power of compassion in his book on altruism:

> When we are mainly concerned with ourselves, we become vulnerable to everything that can affect us. Trapped in this state of mind, egocentric contemplation of the suffering of others undermines our courage; it is felt as a burden that only increases our distress. In the case of compassion, on the other hand, altruistic contemplation of others' suffering greatly increases our courage, our readiness, and our determination to remedy these torments.
>
> (Ricard, 2018, p 49)

Empathic concern is a super-power because it is a form of empathy that does not seem to lead to fatigue or distress, and it is an energy that is directed towards another rather than ourselves. Empathy gives you the information, and compassion motivates action. Ricard has been involved in research participating in studies in a neuroscience laboratory in the US that looked at what is going on in the brain when people feel empathy (cognitive or affective), or compassion. The brain patterns that are usually activated in the brain when feeling empathy correlate with brain patterns that show a negative response from pain. The networks that were activated when Ricard felt compassion to another were those that are usually associated with a positive response. Compassion fatigue was shown not to exist.

> Empathising with the suffering of others is associated with negative states, distress, and activations in brain networks that play a crucial role in empathy for pain. Conversely, compassion is accompanied by positive feelings of warmth and concern for the other and increased activation of brain networks related to reward and affiliation.
>
> (Colonnello et al, 2017)

Compassion is not a word that is used in the workplace very much, although in recent years with the greater focus on well-being in the workplace kindness is more commonly spoken of, which is similar to compassion. Self-compassion is an equally important skill for your own well-being and performance, and we will explore that in the resilience chapter. Building empathic concern at work can enhance your positive relationships through your understanding of others and motivation to want others to feel well and happy.

SELF-AWARENESS

The third vital skill in building positive relationships is self-awareness. Being self-aware means we can notice and understand our own behaviour in relation to others. We are aware of how we communicate and build relationships with other people.

Self-Awareness is having a clear perception of your personality, including your strengths, weaknesses, thoughts, beliefs, motives, and feelings.

(Drigas and Papoutsi, 2018)

The more aware we are, the more we are able to build positive relationships as we know how our behaviour impacts on others. Self-awareness is sometimes described as the very first step to being emotionally intelligent. One of the reasons coaching is such an effective process is because it helps enable greater self-awareness in the person being coached. I have always been fascinated by the paradox of change – when people allow themselves to be fully in touch with who they currently are, it is only then that change can happen. I believe this is a fundamental reason why coaching works. I love the metaphor that comes from acceptance and commitment therapy that describes someone walking on ice and only being able to move forward when they ensure a firm footing.

The more self-aware we are, the more able we are to build lasting positive relationships. One of the ways managers try to build self-awareness in their teams is through giving feedback. The person then knows their development areas and can work on improving them, and also their strengths. But this is just one small way we can improve self-awareness. Others include self-reflection and building a diverse network of relationships. These elements help to build self-awareness in regard to how we interact with others, how we manage our thoughts and our emotions.

Combining empathy, compassion and self-awareness means we can develop positive relationships in a conducive environment and also when the relationships, environments or circumstances are difficult.

Importantly, what follows empathy, compassion and self-awareness is action. It is the action that generates the positive relationships between you and another, as that is what the other person notices and appreciates. When you have empathy you can act with knowledge, when you have compassion you can act with care and kindness, and when you have self-awareness you act with sensitivity and emotional intelligence.

POSITIVE LEADERSHIP

Leaders play a key role in generating positive energy to build positive relationships at work. Kim Cameron, a professor in the US, is recognised as a thought leader in positive relational energy at work, especially in regard to workplace culture and leadership. He has studied the relational positive energy to understand its effect and how to enable it. His research shows that there is a significant relationship between an organisation's performance and the organisation's virtuousness (integrity, optimism and compassion) (Cameron, 2011). Of course, when Cameron refers to organisations' integrity, optimism and compassion, what he is referring to is the behaviour of the people within the organisations (including the leaders). It is the people who decide the organisational processes and create the culture through their behaviour. Therefore, an organisation's virtuousness is really about the sum of the behaviour of the people who work within it and the direction from the leaders of the organisation on *how* they want people to behave and *what* they would like them to work on.

Cameron describes four distinct opportunities for generating relational positive energy at work as a leader. First, by building a positive culture through a strengths-based approach to managing people (we explored strengths in Chapter 3) and having positive expectations and empowering individuals and teams. Second, through understanding the power of reciprocity – doing good or virtuous acts for others so they do good for you. Third, by focusing on positive communication – verbal, written and in the way performance conversations happen. And lastly through positive meaning (we explore meaning more comprehensively in the next chapter), through defining values, encouraging self-leadership and thinking about legacy.

A helpful metaphor to understand positive leadership is the idea of plants turning towards the light to grow and thrive in the sunshine. The idea of turning towards the light applies far more broadly than just to plants – every living thing has a tendency to turn towards the light, and this is called the heliotropic effect. As a leader, if you provide that positive energy you are providing the light, the sunshine, to grow teams and businesses.

How can you as a leader be a positive energiser? Cameron gives some high-level examples: helping people flourish without expecting a return, solving problems, inspiring others, trusting and being trusted, forgiving mistakes and installing confidence in others. What is crucial from Cameron's research is that it shows positive relational energy is not an abstract concept in the workplace; it can be translated into a clear set of behaviours that are tangible and can be developed and even measured to see progress.

GROWING POSITIVE RELATIONSHIPS IN THE WORKPLACE

We have covered how critical positive relationships are, and the positive energy between people that drives positive interactions, so let's now understand how we can practically apply these ideas in the workplace. We will explore what actions we can take to develop positive relationships.

Map your positive energy network

A useful place to start when looking to increase your own positive relationships and reflect on the impact your emotions and behaviours are having on others is to do a positive energy network map. This exercise helps you to consider all the people in your network at work, and outside of work, if you want to include a wider circle, and where the positive energy is coming from. It is also useful to bear in mind that no working relationship is an isolated relationship, everyone and everything is networked. The relationship you build with someone affects the relationships you can build with others. Aim to build a network of people that motivate and inspire you and that you motivate and inspire.

INDIVIDUAL PPI

Positive energy map

Take a blank sheet of paper and write your name in the middle of the page. Now brainstorm all of the people who you most closely work with. These can be team members, managers, suppliers, stakeholders, mentors, peers, colleagues, clients. If you interact with a team of people and know them collectively rather than individually, then you can have that team as one on the map.

Now draw individual arrows between you and each other person. Arrows towards the others show the positive energy you give to that person. The arrows that come back to you illustrate the positive energy that person gives back to you. The thicker the arrow, the stronger the positive energy. The thinner the arrow, the weaker the positivity. You can also give a mark out of 10 for how positive that person makes you feel: 10 is the most positive, 1 the least. To help decide on the arrows and scores, ask yourself, when you interact with that person, how does it affect your energy levels?

The second step in this exercise involves seeking feedback. You can ask key people on your network map, out of 10 how much do you energise them? This means you can populate the scores for the arrows going away from you.

Now reflect.

- Who gives you the most positive energy? What do they do to show this? How could you do more of what they do?
- Who gives you the least positive energy? What do they do to show this? What could you do less of to ensure you are not de-energising others?
- How could you increase your daily positive interactions with others in your organisation?

You can also re-do this exercise but change the meaning of the arrows. This time draw the arrows according to how much support you give that other person, and how much support they give you. The thicker the arrow the more support.

Now reflect.

- How comfortable are you with your support map? Is the equilibrium comfortable for you (the amount of support you give and the amount you receive)?
- What would you like to change on your map?

Develop empathy

Developing empathy cannot be done in a room alone, it needs to be developed and practised with others. There are two important ways to do this. The first way is to enhance your curiosity. Without genuine curiosity in other people you will struggle to develop empathy as conversations lack authenticity. Curiosity motivates you to want to ask questions, want to listen. Curiosity makes you want to find out what you have in common with someone that can fuel conversations on shared experiences and opinions. Some people have a natural curiosity. Many well-known geniuses were highly curious – Albert Einstein, Leonardo da Vinci and Archimedes were all curious about the world. Whether you are naturally curious or not about people, it is entirely possible to practise and develop curiosity to enable you to build empathy to underpin your positive relationships at work.

Although some people are more similar to ourselves than others – and we have a natural interest in those who are more similar – being curious about those who are more dissimilar helps develop empathy as we begin to understand those who do not see the world as we do (and all the value that brings). Trying to find some common ground with them gives you a goal in being curious, and a conversation starter each time you see them.

When you find this common ground, this is gold dust for your working relationship. It helps you build rapport and get the conversation going. The more common ground you can find with them, the more material you have to develop conversations with them and the more they will have rapport with you.

Curiosity enables you to smile, ask questions and listen well, naturally. By appearing natural you build trust more quickly and effectively. Curiosity has far more benefits than just improving your working relationships. People who have a good level of curiosity have also been shown to have higher levels of satisfaction with their lives (Kashdan and Silvia, 2009).

Stumm, a psychologist who has done research into this area, believes '*that curiosity may be the single best predictor of individual success because it incorporates intelligence, persistence, and hunger for novelty in one*' (Leslie, 2014).

TOP TIPS

Develop your curiosity

Give yourself a jolt – do something slightly or very differently than you would normally do. For example:

- sitting in a different carriage on the train;
- having coffee with someone you would not normally chat to;
- working in a different room;
- calling up an old colleague or friend just to reconnect;
- walking a different route to work;
- running a different route.

Aim to find common ground with someone you do not know that well and build a conversation around that common ground.

The second way to develop more empathy is to focus on your listening skills at work. There are different types of listening (Thomson, 2009). The first is not listening at all – someone is talking, and you aren't listening (or you are pretending to listen). The next is waiting for a pause in the conversation so you can speak (or leave), which is tolerating. Social conversations can often be like this, with people wanting to share, but not necessarily really listening to what the other person said. The next is listening to analyse, whether you agree or disagree, and you can provide your own views – a really useful listening tool when debating ideas at work. The next is listening to empathise. You listen not only to understand what the other person is saying but why they are saying it, you seek to understand them. An advanced type of listening involves empathising and aiming to raise the awareness of the other person to understand more about themselves in the context of the topic they were talking about (this is the type of listening used in coaching). This type of listening is for the other person's gain. To listen in this way you will need to ask open questions and reflect back or summarise the other person's thoughts.

Table 4.3 Types of listening

Ignoring	Not paying attention
Tolerating	Waiting to speak
Analysing	Agreeing, disagreeing or debating
Understanding for self	Listening to understand
Understanding for others	Listening to help the other person understand more about themselves

All these types of listening have their place in the workplace, and we may use a blend of them in any one conversation. You may need to analyse ideas, thoughts, plans and strategies. You may need to ignore disruptions, or negativity. Importantly for the topic of this chapter, building positive relationships at work, the last two types of listening help build empathy and compassion – you are seeking to understand others, and seeking to support others.

It is the last type of listening that is particularly useful for helping to develop empathy as it is focused on the other person – the '*why*' of listening is all about helping the other person to explore. The more you listen with this mindset, the more you have the opportunity to really find out about someone else and what is in their head. There is no greater way to develop empathy. Focus on listening in this way when you have one-to-one conversations with your colleagues and team members.

Listening skills

Put the team into pairs and assign one person as the talker, and one the listener. The person who is talking needs to talk about something that is happening at work that is an issue for them. This could be something specific to the work they do, or more generally about their own development. They need to talk about this for 10 minutes within their pair. The person listening has the remit of listening to help the other person reflect on their issue to find a way forward (this is the type of listening a coach does).

The challenge is that the listener is only allowed to:

- ask questions;
- reflect back the person's exact words;
- summarise.

They are not allowed to add their own experiences, give advice or change topic.

Once the 10 minutes is done you swap the team around and the other person is now the listener. You can also swap pairs and do this twice more.

At the end of the four listening sessions there is a debrief.

- When being the listener, how did you find only being able to ask questions, reflect and summarise?
- How do you think you supported the other person?
- What did you do to show listening?
- How did you help the other person reflect on their issue?
- How could you use this learning in your conversations at work with team members?
- When being listened to, how did the conversation help you with you issue?
- How did you know the other person was listening?
- How could you use the experience today at work with your team members?

Grow compassion

How can you feel more warm towards others to develop positive relationships? How can you step out of your own skin and want to support others in a positive way? Charities must activate compassion as they need us to donate to their causes. They often use real stories in their marketing to grab our attention and make the suffering real. We are all familiar with the charity nights on TV interspersed with celebrities to entertain us and real stories of people suffering. How does this relate to the workplace? What the charities are doing is helping us to care by making the issues real. At work we want people to care about their own responsibilities, care about their teammates, care about the culture and vision of the organisation. Once people care, they are much more likely to act. We also want to care, about our work and about others.

What we focus on grows in our minds. When we see kindness in the world, then kindness grows. When we see laughter, laughter grows, but if we see fear, or anger, or sadness, then this grows too. If you have always been quite competitive, it is likely that rivalry has grown, and you see it everywhere. Of course, these other emotions are important, but what we are looking at here is how to be more compassionate, and therefore how to cultivate it. So we need to notice it. Positive psychologists maintain that noticing kindness in others is a brilliant way to enhance your compassion for others.

Top tips on how to grow compassion in yourself and in others

- Assume good intent. If you start from the basis that people usually mean well in their actions, then this helps you approach communicating them with curiosity and warmth, even if they have disagreed with you, or caused conflict.
- Understand the power of reciprocation. When you do a good deed for someone, then they feel indebted to you and want to do a good deed back. This is the power of reciprocation. The deed does not need to be particularly big – it can be just buying a coffee, or offering to support an idea in a meeting. In fact, the small nature of the deed motivates the person even more to want to return the good deed. By choosing to do an unexpected good deed for someone at work, the person will want to do a good deed back. This helps nurture positivity and kindness for others.

Increase self-awareness

In the 1950s two American psychologists devised a model that aimed to assess and improve relationships with others. Their names were Joseph Luft and Harry Ingham, and the model combined their two names to be known as the Johari Window (Luft and Ingham, 1955). Using the ideas from this model is one way to increase self-awareness. The window has four panels within it, known as regions or arenas. The first window is what you know about yourself, and what others know too – called the open arena. This could be behaviour, feelings, knowledge, experience. The aim in teams is to open the open arena as much as possible so that trust can be built from knowledge of each other. When you have a new team, or new team members in an existing team, this area will be smaller as it takes time to know people. The ideal Johari Window has a large open arena.

The second window is what others know about you but you are not aware of yourself. This is called the blind spot – similar to the blind spot in a car wing mirror. The only way to see what is in your blind spot is by seeking feedback from others. You can also encourage others to reduce their blind spot by offering feedback and encouraging others to seek feedback.

The third arena is the hidden area, the things you know about yourself but keep hidden from others. You can reduce the size of this arena by disclosing to others information about yourself, your thoughts, feelings, experience and knowledge. You can also encourage others to reduce their hidden area by encouraging them to share their ideas, and build trust so people feel confortable to share parts of their hidden area with you.

The last arena is the unknown. This is what you don't know about yourself, and what others also do not know. This could be an ability you don't know you have through lack of opportunity or repressed feelings or experiences.

To increase your self-awareness you need to increase the open arena, and decrease the hidden arena and blind spot. You can do this by:

- seeking feedback;
- disclosing your thoughts/feelings/experience/knowledge.

To help colleagues and team members increase their self-awareness you can:

- encourage them to seek feedback;
- give feedback to them;
- build trust so that they feel they can disclose their hidden arena.

Table 4.4 The Johari Window adapted from Joseph Luft and Harry Ingham

Open arena	**Blind spot**
Thoughts, feelings, experience, knowledge that you know and others know	What others know about you but you do not know yourself
Hidden arena	**Unknown**
What you keep hidden from others	What you do not know about yourself and what others do not know about you

The concept of '*giving feedback*' at work is usually more associated with giving negative feedback than positive. To build positive relationships at work, one simple way to decrease someone else's blind spot, increase their open arena and generate positive relational energy is to give more positive feedback than developmental feedback to colleagues, managers and team members. We often only feel compelled to give feedback when things are going wrong. We assume what is going right must be in the other person's open arena, but often it is not. Being given positive feedback increases self-awareness and motivation, and is self-perpetuating, as once we feel we are good at something, we tend to do more of it and put more effort in.

SUMMARY CHECKLIST

To develop positive relationships at work:

- map your positive energy network;
- develop a particular type of listening skill – listening to help the other person understand more about themselves;
- develop your curiosity, particularly for people who think differently to you;
- consciously notice kindness in the workplace (what we focus on grows) and do kind deeds for others to activate the power of reciprocation;
- grow your self-awareness through asking for feedback and giving feedback openly, especially when positive;
- give positive feedback to others.

REFLECTIONS

If you asked someone to name a memory at work that brought them joy, then I am almost certain they would name a memory that involved other people. When we feel part of a group or community, or friendship, then the joy we create is so much more memorable and meaningful. What is your favourite memory at work in the last 12 months?

A hidden but crucial part of building positive relationships with others at work is the relationship we have with ourselves at work. Do you empathise with yourself and understand why you act how you do? Do you show yourself kindness and compassion, even when you don't meet your own expectations? Do you give yourself the time to reflect on your own behaviour and actions and appreciate how they impact on others? When you have a positive relationship with yourself it is so much easier to have a positive relationship with others and be happy for others when things are going well, and supportive for others when things are not. We need to work on building a positive relationship with how we are with ourselves, as well as how we are with others. What is your self-talk like? Self-talk is what we say to ourselves in our heads, our inner voice. Do you encourage, congratulate, comfort and support yourself? This is the place to start when building positive relationships.

When people come to coaching searching for presence, gravitas or confidence, the place to start is always building a positive relationship with themselves.

Someone who has presence is someone who has interest, curiosity and kindness for others and themselves. Taking the summary checklist actions and applying them to yourself is a great place to start: do you energise yourself, do you listen to yourself to understand (not to judge), are you curious about your thoughts or actions, or judgemental and punishing, do you notice kindness in yourself and do you give yourself positive feedback? As happiness exists between people as well as within people, it only makes sense to cultivate it from the inside out and the outside in.

SELF-COACHING QUESTIONS

Work through GROW for this topic and do add more questions/reflections at each stage than are detailed here if you want to explore further.

Goal (to uncover what your aim is)

- What specifically would I like to improve with regard to:
  - my relationships at work?
  - my relationship with myself?
  - my team's relationships at work?
  - my organisation's business relationships (for business owners and senior leadership teams)?

Reality (to understand)

- What is going on for me and or my team that makes this something I would like to change?
- What could I do to understand more about my own behaviour at work and how it is perceived?
- How positive are my relationships at work out of 10 (where 10 is the most positive and 1 the least)? Where would I like that number to be?

Options (to explore)

- What could I do to improve relationships at work for myself and for my team?
- How could I use the skill of empathy to improve my relationships at work?
- Who, apart from myself, needs to make a change in my team?
- If me or my team had exceptionally positive relationships at work what would we be doing differently?

Will (to decide on action)

- What actions will I take?
- What is the first step I will take and when?
- What deadlines will I set for myself?

REFERENCES

Ahuvia, A, Thin, N, Haybron, D M, Biswas-Diener, R, Ricard, M and Timsit, J (2015) Happiness: An Interactionist Perspective. *International Journal of Wellbeing*, 5(1): 1–18. doi: 10.5502/ijw.v5i1.1.

Basford, T E and Offermann, L R (2012) Beyond Leadership: The Impact of Co-worker Relationships on Employee Motivation and Intent to Stay. *Journal of Management & Organization*, 18(6): 807–17. doi: 10.5172/jmo.2012.18.6.807.

Bourg Carter, S (2012) Emotions Are Contagious: Choose Your Company Wisely. *Psychology Today*. [online] Available at: www.psychologytoday.com/us/blog/high-octane-women/201210/emotions-are-contagious-choose-your-company-wisely (accessed 7 March 2023).

Byham, W C and Cox, J (1991) *Zapp! The Lightning of Empowerment*. London: Century Business.

Cameron, K, Mora, C, Leutscher, L and Calarco, M (2011) Effects of Positive Practices on Organizational Effectiveness. *Journal of Applied Behavioral Science*, 47(3): 266–308.

Christakis, N A and Fowler, J H (2009) *Connected: The Surprising Power of our Social Networks and How they Shape our Lives*. New York: Little, Brown.

Cohen, S and Wills, T A (1985) Stress, Social Support, and the Buffering Hypothesis. *Psychological Bulletin*, 98(2): 310–57. doi: 10.1037/0033-2909.98.2.310.

Colonnelo, V, Petrocchi, N, Farinelli, M and Ottavian, C (2017) Positive Social Interactions in a Lifespan Perspective with a Focus on Opioidergic and Oxytocinergic Systems: Implications for Neuroprotection. *Current Neuropharmacology*, 15: 543–61. [online] Available at: www.ncbi.nlm.nih.gov/pmc/articles/PMC5543675/pdf/CN-15-543.pdf (accessed 7 March 2023).

Dowling, T (2018) Compassion Does Not Fatigue! *Canadian Veterinary Journal*, 59(7): 749–50. [online] Available at: www.ncbi.nlm.nih.gov/pmc/articles/PMC6005077/ (accessed 7 March 2023).

Drigas, A S and Papoutsi, C (2018) A New Layered Model on Emotional Intelligence. *Behavioral Sciences*, 8(5): 45. doi: 10.3390/bs8050045.

Fredrickson, B (2011) *Positivity*. London: Oneworld.

Herrando, C and Constantinidis, E (2021) Emotional Contagion: A Brief Overview and Future Directions. *Frontiers in Psychology*, 12. doi: 10.3389/fpsyg.2021.712606.

Kashdan, T B and Silvia, P J (2009) Curiosity and Interest: The Benefits of Thriving on Novelty and Challenge. In Lopez, S J and Snyder, C R (eds) *Oxford Handbook of Positive Psychology* (pp 367–74). Oxford: Oxford University Press.

Leslie, I (2014) *Curious: The Desire to Know and Why Your Future Depends on It*. New York: Basic Books.

Luft, J and Ingham, H (1955) The Johari Window: A Graphic Model of Interpersonal Awareness. *Proceedings of the Western Training Laboratory in Group Development*. Los Angeles, CA: UCLA.

Mertika, A, Mitskidou, P and Stalikas, A (2020) 'Positive Relationships' and their Impact on Wellbeing: A Review of Current Literature. *Psychology: The Journal of the Hellenic Psychological Society*, 25(1): 115–27. doi: 10.12681/psy_hps.25340.

Morrison, R and Nolan, T (2007) Negative Relationships in the Workplace: A Qualitative Study. *Qualitative Research in Accounting & Management*, 4(3): 203–21. doi: 10.1108/11766090710826646.

Moynihan, D and Pandey, S (2008) The Ties That Bind: Social Networks, Person-Organization Value Fit, and Turnover Intention. *Journal of Public Administration Research and Theory*, 18(2): 205–27. doi: 10.1093/jopart/mum013.

Nolan, T and Küpers, W (2009) Organizational Climate, Organizational Culture and Workplace Relationships. In Morrison, R L and Wright, S L (eds), *Friends and Enemies in Organizations* (pp 57–77). London: Palgrave Macmillan.

Oh, H, Chung, M H and Labianca, G (2004) Group Social Capital and Group Effectiveness: The Role of Informal Socializing Ties. *Academy of Management Journal*, 47(6): 860–75.

Peterson, C (2008) Other People Matter: Two Examples. *Psychology Today*. [online] Available at: www.psychologytoday.com/intl/blog/the-good-life/200806/other-people-matter-two-examples (accessed 7 March 2023).

Ricard, M (2018) *Altruism: The Science and Psychology of Kindness*. London: Atlantic Books.

Society for Human Resource Management (2016) *Employee Job Satisfaction and Employee Report.* [online] Available at: www.shrm.org/hr-today/trends-and-forecasting/research-and-surveys/documents/2016-employee-job-satisfaction-and-engagement-report.pdf (accessed 7 March 2023).

Thomson, B (2009) *Don't Just do Something, Sit There.* Oxford: Chandos Publishing.

Wang, X-H F, Fang, Y, Qureshi, I and Janssen, O (2015) Understanding Employee Innovative Behaviour: Integrating the Social Network and Leader-Member Exchange Perspectives. *Journal of Organizational Behavior*, 36(3): 403–20. doi: 10.1002/job.1994.

5

Finding meaning

If you know the why you can live any how.

(Frankl, 2004)

In this chapter we will explore the M of PERMA – meaning – and how an increase in meaning at work increases well-being and performance. Meaning is about having a sense of purpose, significance and coherence. As positive psychology is the study of what makes life worth living, meaning is crucial to positive psychology as it is a key component of this. There has been a noticeable increasing desire for meaning at work in the last 30 years. A survey in the US of over 1000 people in 2020 found that contributing to society and creating meaningful work were the top two priorities of employees (McKinsey Quarterly, 2020).

UNDERSTANDING HAPPINESS AND MEANING

Seligman, the psychologist who popularised positive psychology, describes happiness in life as having three components. The first component is 'The Pleasant Life', the idea of which is originally attributed to the Greek philosopher Aristippus, dating far back to the fourth century BC. The pleasant life is about finding happiness by doing things you enjoy that bring you pleasure and positivity, such as eating good food, meeting friends, doing enjoyable hobbies. You can have a pleasant life by savouring the happy experiences and feeling grateful for them. The happiness these experiences bring is described as hedonic happiness. The happiness that we can have from these experiences, though, is transient and is subject to 'hedonic adaptation', sometimes called the hedonic treadmill. Hedonic adaptation is the dulling of the joy from doing something many times, or the dulling of the appreciation we feel for something. Over time, after experiencing something pleasurable our baseline level of pleasure from that experience returns to where it was before. For example, in your career you may have previously felt incredibly happy when being offered a new role or a pay rise. Over time, however, the feeling of happiness gradually becomes a feeling of neutrality, and you start to compare the current role or pay with something better. If we just rely on hedonic happiness for our well-being, then life and work can be an exhausting search for enjoyable events to be grateful for and savour.

The second is 'The Good Life', which is finding happiness through understanding your strengths and virtues and using them in your life. This idea also originated in the fourth century BC, from Aristotle. He put forward the idea that happiness in life also comes from the feeling that life has value beyond just feeling pleasure from enjoying happy times. The joy that we have from using strengths and working in line with our values is much more long lasting than the joy from a fun time.

The third component builds on this idea further and is called 'The Meaningful Life'. The meaningful life is about using your strengths and passions, but this time for the benefit of others rather than your own benefit. Both the good life and the meaningful life build eudemonic happiness which is happiness from meaning and purpose. Crucially, eudemonic adaptation doesn't exist. The happiness we gain from using our strengths in the service of ourselves or others does not return our happiness levels to baseline – we don't adapt to that joy or get numbed from it – as it does from hedonic pleasures. Eudemonic happiness is much more powerful for long-term feelings of purpose, significance and coherence. It is useful to think about meaning being a long-term investment you make for happiness. An investment that you regularly contribute to, and you can withdraw from a little now and then, that builds over time, and gives direction, a framework, sense of impact and comfort in your life.

While having meaning helps with long-term happiness, this does not imply that you can't find meaning every day. Having meaning is like ripples in a pool of water. The meaning may stem from the simple act of happiness it gives from the satisfaction from doing an action at work using your strengths: the first small ripple of water. Meaning also can come from the impact the work has on the team: a larger ripple in the pool. Or meaning may come from the impact the work has on the business, the sector, the community or the industry: the larger ripples that expand out into the pool reaching out, having a far-reaching impact. Therefore, meaning can be found in everyday activities, and in longer-term pursuits.

When we 'make meaning' we look at what has happened or what is going to happen and appraise the event to understand the positive or beneficial aspect of it; this is called 'benefit finding'. We also strive to make sense of events or a series of events, which is 'sense making'. Despite the extensive challenges the pandemic created and terrible impact of Covid-19, it is very common to hear people talk about the positives of being in lockdown, such as family time, less commuting, the rise in home working, fewer cars on the road, which is benefit finding, and hearing people trying the make sense of why it happened. Benefit finding and sense-making help us to create meaning from events or a series of events that have happened or are going to happen.

Present events have meaning because of their relationship to future events. Many metaphors for the meaning of life reflect this: life as a journey, a script or a destination. There is no physical connection between the tasks we do now and the future, but purpose connects the current action with a future achievement. I have lost count of the number of times clients have endured stressful times of high workload due to the work being linked to a greater purpose – their growth and development in their careers, or their purpose of providing for their families, or for a particular ambition they want to reach. Purpose means they can endure what would otherwise be untenable.

THE FOUR NEEDS FOR MEANING

Having meaning in the workplace is usually referred to as 'meaningful work'. This is 'the global judgement that one's work accomplishes significant, valuable, or worthwhile goals that are congruent with one's existential values' (Allan et al, 2018).

How we derive meaning at work can be broken down into four needs that must be met: purpose, values, efficacy and self-worth (Baumeister and Vohs, 2001).

Purpose

The first is *purpose* – a reason for being here or doing something. When we have a reason for doing something this gives us motivation, and we need motivation to grow, learn, work and achieve. Purpose connects the activities we do now to the future and to the world outside of ourselves. I have worked with many people in coaching to support them in finding purpose in their working lives. People don't always use the word purpose, though; they may say, '*I want to have more impact*', or '*I want to feel like there is a direction to where I am heading*' or '*I want to understand why I have made these decisions, and what I want to do next*'. All of these desires link back to having purpose. I have also seen leaders who have a strong sense of purpose, who struggle to understand why their team members don't have that same sense of purpose. They report frustrations with their team members' supposed lack of motivation or dedication. In these situations, there can be a misalignment of purpose between the leader and the team.

With purpose comes the '*Why*', and most often the why is something that you are working towards in the future – a goal. Frankl describes how the prisoners in the concentration camp he was imprisoned in during the Second World War who lost faith in the future were doomed. This was illustrated in an unusually high death rate from illness in the prisoners between Christmas and New Year at the end of 1944; Frankl explains that the reason for this was that many gave up hope. They had held on with the belief in the future that they would be home by Christmas. When this did not happen, they lost faith in the future, and gave up mentally fighting to survive. The '*why*' to survive was no longer there (Frankl, 2004).

Values

The second need is *values.* Values give us a measure of how we feel we should be behaving and living, what feels right and what feels wrong. A value is a principle or standard of behaviour. They are what we consider important in our lives and we measure our behaviour according to those values. For example, kindness is a value, or family, or health or wealth. Values give us a sense of safety and shared understanding with others. When a team is clear on the common values they all hold, this is a powerful enabler for high work performance.

By living life according to your values, you minimise feelings of guilt, anxiety and regret, as you can feel more secure that your actions are in line with your beliefs (Baumeister and Vohs, 2001). Baumeister and Vohs suggest that the component of meaning most difficult to achieve in modern life is meaning through values. They suggest that in modern society values based on tradition and religion have been weakened, with no consensus on their replacement.

Efficacy

The third need for meaning is the feeling of having *efficacy*: '*A life that had purpose and values but no efficacy would be tragic: The person might know what was desirable but could not do anything with that knowledge*' (Baumeister and Vohs, 2001). Efficacy is having the feeling that you can make a difference. Having efficacy gives people a sense of control over their working lives with the belief of '*I can do this*' despite constant change and challenge. Life is not stable, we are changing constantly all the time, as are the people around us. Meaning is about making connections between distinct things that do not have a physical connection, which is unique to humans. We have a human desire for stability and overlaying meaning onto our day-to-day lives enables us to manage the changes we see all the time through our feeling of efficacy (being able to make a difference).

In the workplace this is a vital insight, as change is a given, and therefore an increase in meaning at work helps people deal with change and even thrive during change. To visualise this, imagine a workplace as the sea; constantly moving, changing, experiencing rocky times, sunny days, with powerful waves. A boat on the sea with a distinct colour, style and route of travel is a boat full of meaning. The boat carries people over a period of change or storms and sails calmly during more steady times. If you can get onto the boat of meaning then you can travel with others who see the same meaning about events, which also creates a constant for you, being able to share meaning with others.

Self-worth

The final need for meaning is *self-worth*, the feeling of having value, being seen and feeling that you matter. Having high self-worth is a great enabler of agency, an ability to feel that you can achieve. The dictionary definition of self-worth is '*a feeling that you are a good person who deserves to be treated with respect*' (Cambridge Dictionary, nd). Low self-worth means low self-belief and low self-esteem. When you have a high sense of self-worth it means you understand that what you achieve, or the talents you have, are not what make you who you are. You are valuable just because you are *you*.

High self-worth is not a high bank account, a high position, a high-flying career, beauty, popularity or the amount of followers you have. Social media can have a devastating impact on self-worth if someone links their self-worth with the idea of being liked or followed. And in turn this impacts the level of meaning in their lives – it can be lower because they equate self-worth with something it is not. Low self-worth can also cause trouble at work if someone believes that their worth is determined by how others relate to them. An over-reliance on others to boost self-worth at work can mean constant disappointment. I often speak to leaders transitioning to more senior roles and encourage them to self-reflect and give themselves positive or negative feedback to grow and learn. This builds self-worth and a sense of control (Ackerman, 2018).

Table 5.1 The four needs for meaning

Components of meaning	
Purpose	An intention to achieve a longer-term goal that is personally meaningful and makes a positive mark on the world outside yourself
Values	Fundamental attitudes and beliefs that guide your behaviour
Efficacy	Confidence in your ability to make a difference
Self-worth	A feeling that you are a good person who deserves to be treated with respect

(Baumeister and Vohs, 2001.)

MEANING AND WELL-BEING

Meaning and well-being are closely linked, and studies have shown a strong correlation between higher meaning and higher well-being. '*The body of evidence regarding meaning is large and growing quickly, and appears to reliably demonstrate the importance of meaning to human wellbeing and flourishing*' (Steger, 2018).

There is no agreed consensus why this is so, but there are two hypotheses. The first is that people who have meaning in their lives have better relationships, which leads to higher well-being. The second is that people who have meaning engage in different activities, such as work that helps others. It is not clear whether meaning is a component of well-being or a pathway to well-being (the end state or a step on the journey). What is clear is that meaning promotes better health and better health promotes meaning. When you consider the four key sources of meaning – purpose, self-worth, values and efficacy – it is easy to imagine how this would impact mental health. If someone had no purpose, low feelings of self-worth, no values to live their life by, and a feeling that they were not able to make a difference, this would be bound to impact on mental health. But studies show physical health is also improved when people have meaning in their lives, including better exercise habits, leading to better physical fitness, and better dietary habits, leading to range of physical health benefits. A number of research studies support this and show how meaning affects different elements of well-being (Steger, 2017).

Table 5.2 Relationship between well-being and meaning

Higher meaning leads to:
Lower levels of perceived stress
Lower anxiety
More frequent feelings of happiness
Longer life
Greater ability to cope during difficult times
Lower depressive symptoms
Better exercise habits
Better dietary habits

(Steger, 2017)

MEANING AND PERFORMANCE

Finding work meaningful is also closely linked to improved performance at work. '*A growing body of research links meaningful work to employee well-being and performance and meaningless work to disengagement and alienation*' (Van Wingerden and Van der Stoep 2018).

If you look at the four sources of meaning, think of them in a work context and imagine not having them, it is again easy to see how meaning relates to performance. If someone has little purpose at work, they will be less motivated and have less direction, with low efficacy they will have less self-belief and willingness to learn and take risks, low self-worth will mean a constant need for others around them to tread carefully and offer only positive feedback, a constant need to be reassured. Lastly, if someone does not live their life according to their personal values then this would show up at work in attitude and inconsistency of effort. There are, of course, values that the organisation or team holds. If someone has little respect for them, then their fit within the team and their dedication to the team's cause is compromised. I have seen people leave roles because their values do not align with the organisation's values. Teams thrive when these are aligned.

Doing meaningful work enables people to have increased job satisfaction, increased commitment to their career, increase in flow and an increased sense of autonomy and ambition. For a team or an organisation, when people do meaningful work there is lower staff turnover, and improved engagement. A recent review showed that meaningful work experiences formed the foundation for employee engagement in organisations (Bailey et al, 2019).

How much is employees having meaning in their work worth to businesses? In one study it was found that people who have very meaningful work spend one extra hour per week working and take two fewer days paid leave (Achor et al, 2018). Meaning equals increased willingness to do more and spend more time at work. Employees who have meaning in their work also have greater work satisfaction, which correlates strongly with productivity. The US-based researchers say that *'Based on established job satisfaction-to-productivity ratios, we estimate that highly meaningful work will generate an additional $9,078 per worker, per year'* (Achor et al, 2018).

Increased meaning at work also means that people are more likely to stay in their jobs. *'There is a clear connection between engagement and retention. The more engaged the workforce, the greater the percent of employees plan on staying with their current employer'* (Towers Perrin, 2012).

An important part of understanding meaningful work is that meaning does not necessarily bring the same kind of joy you have from hedonic pleasures, such as a lovely lunch, a great team day, a team night out, increased pay. To illustrate this think about work such as healthcare, which is often a vocation. It can involve long hours and be tiring, emotionally exhausting and even heart-breaking. But it is rewarding, motivating and meaningful. The difficulties are worth the meaning, thankfully, for many people who choose these professions.

> *Living with meaning and purpose is not easy. It may not make us happy in the moment. It requires self-reflection, effort, getting our hands dirty, and struggling with problems that can make us feel frustrated and inadequate.*
>
> (Duncan, 2018)

CREATING MEANING AT WORK

How can you ensure you have meaning in your work, and how can you help others to have meaning at work? You can't make other people find meaning and you can't change what people find meaningful. You also can't make yourself find meaning or be given meaning by others. The paradox of meaning is that research shows that if we actively seek it as a goal in itself that can actually make us more unhappy, in the same way that actively seeking '*being happy*' can make us more unhappy. Meaning needs to be a longer-term happy outcome of the actions we take, rather than a goal in itself. Feeling pressure to have meaning is actually stressful and feeling like there should be a '*meaning to life*' is also unhelpful, as there is not one meaning to life. Many things make life meaningful.

Therefore, if you are looking to increase meaning for yourself or your team it is about understanding yourself (your values and purpose), developing your self-efficacy and self-worth, and also appreciating the four sources of meaning in others to create the awareness and the environment that enables you or others to find meaning in the present and over time.

ENABLING MEANINGFUL WORK

Let's explore practical ideas we can use in the workplace to increase meaning both for ourselves and for others that enable meaning by providing one of the sources of meaning: values, purpose, efficacy and self-worth.

Knowing your values

Knowing your values helps you to understand what is important to you, what you need to prioritise and also why you can feel angry or anxious when an event or a person compromises your values.

INDIVIDUAL PPI

Values exercise

Look at the list of values included here and choose up to 16 of them that are important to you. You can also choose values that are not listed here, it is not a definitive list of values. Write each one on a separate Post-it note or small card/ piece of paper. Split them into two piles randomly. Take the top two from each pile and ask yourself which is more important to you. Put the lesser value aside. Do the same for the rest of the pack. You should be left with up to eight values. Check the discarded pile and put any back on that you feel should be in your top six. If you now have 12 or more, repeat the exercise of asking which is more important to you. You are aiming for five to six top values.

Once you have your top five to six, lay them out in front of you in an arrangement that makes sense to you. This may be a circle, a line or a pattern. Then ask yourself these questions for each value.

- Out of five, how much am I honouring this value currently? (Where five is fully honouring and one is hardly honouring at all.)
- Out of five, how much would I like to honour this value?
- What would I need to change in my life and work to honour this value more?

Accomplishment	Excitement	Patriotism
Accountability	Expertise	Peace
Accuracy	Exploration	Perfection
Achievement	Expressiveness	Positivity
Acknowledgement	Fairness	Practicality
Adventurousness	Faith	Preparedness
Altruism	Family	Presence
Ambition	Fidelity	Productivity
Assertiveness	Fitness	Professionalism
Authenticity	Flexibility	Prudence
Awareness	Focus	Purpose
Balance	Forgiveness	Recognition
Beauty	Freedom	Relationships
Belonging	Fun	Reliability
Boldness	Generosity	Resourcefulness
Calmness	Gentleness	Respect
Carefulness	Goodness	Restraint
Challenge	Grace	Romance
Cheerfulness	Growth	Safety
Collaboration	Happiness	Security
Commitment	Harmony	Self-actualisation
Community	Health	Self-control
Compassion	Helpfulness	Selflessness
Competitiveness	Holiness	Self-reliance
Confidence	Honesty	Sensitivity
Consistency	Honour	Serenity
Contentment	Humility	Service
Continuous improvement	Humour	Simplicity
Contribution	Independence	Speed
Control	Ingenuity	Spirituality
Cooperation	Innovation	Spontaneity
Correctness	Insightfulness	Stability
Courage	Integrity	Strength
Courtesy	Intelligence	Structure
Creativity	Intellectual status	Success
Curiosity	Intuition	Support
Decisiveness	Irreverence	Tact
Dependability	Joy	Teamwork
Determination	Justice	Temperance
Diligence	Kindness	Thankfulness
Discipline	Laughter	Thoroughness
Discovery	Leadership	Thoughtfulness
Discretion	Learning	Tolerance
Diversity	Legacy	Tradition
Dynamism	Listening	Trustworthiness
Ease	Love	Truth
Effectiveness	Loyalty	Understanding
Efficiency	Making a difference	Uniqueness
Effortlessness	Mastery	Unity
Empathy	Obedience	Usefulness
Empowerment	Openness	Vision
Engagement	Optimism	Vitality
Enjoyment	Order	Wealth
Enthusiasm	Originality	Wisdom
Equality	Passion	
Excellence	Patience	

TEAM PPI

Values exercise

Each person works in a pair to find their individual top three values and answers these questions.

- What are your top three values in the workplace?
- How supportive is the team environment in helping you honour your three values? (Mark each out of five.)
- What would need *to be* different at work for you to be able to honour each value in the workplace more?
- What would you need *to do* differently to be able to honour that value more at work?

Each pair can then share two key insights from their pair discussion with the team. The team can agree actions to increase values-based meaning for the team by answering these questions.

- What do we need to stop doing?
- What do we need to start doing?
- What do we need to do more of?
- What do we need to do less of?

Understanding *ikigai*

The Japanese concept of *ikigai* means your reason for being: what brings you joy in life, inspires you and brings you purpose. '*Iki*' means '*life*' in Japanese and '*gai*' means '*value*' or '*worth*'. People have *ikigai* if they do something they love that they are good at, that they can be paid for and that contributes in some way to others. This concept is often used for people who are searching for their next career step and want to find more meaning in their work. The idea of *ikigai* is about having purpose.

Ikigai includes four concepts.

- *What you love*
- *What you are good at*
- *What you can be paid for*
- *What the world needs*

(Garcia and Miralles, 2017)

Finding your *ikigai*

You can use the idea of *ikigai* for career planning when reflecting on each of the areas to uncover what is meaningful for you.

What you love

- What do you most enjoy doing at work?
- What would you like to do for work if there were no restrictions or barriers?
- When have you been most happy at work and what were you doing?

What you are good at

- What are your strengths?
- What do other people say that you are good at?
- What positive adjectives would your colleagues use to describe you?
- What do people come to you for advice on?

What you can be paid for

- What level of wealth do you require for the financial needs you must satisfy (outgoings and dependants)?
- What roles interest you that can match the pay you would like to have?
- What is your financial target for income in the next three years and what career moves could satisfy that?

What the world needs

- Is there demand in the marketplace for the type of role you would like to do?
- Will this work be needed in the future (5–10 years from now)?
- Are other people successful in this role?

This approach can also be used to find fulfilment and purpose within a role you are already in or for finding new roles or completely different opportunities. You can reflect on what aspects of the role you like the most and shape the role into one that gives you more *ikigai*.

You can also use these questions to think about what you enjoy outside of working. We don't need to find our *ikigai* just in work but can build a life of purpose with what we do inside and outside of work.

More than yourself

Deeper meaning is found when we think outside of ourselves. People find more meaning in their working lives when they can see that what they are doing is benefiting something much bigger than their own well-being, or their own achievements. Steger describes three layers of meaning, the first being meaning found by understanding your purpose at work from clear roles and responsibilities. The second layer of meaning is that the work sits in harmony with your personal life. And third, that meaning is felt when you do work that benefits others or is for the greater good. Positive psychologists call this positive altruism, when the '*altruistic behaviour increases the welfare of both the benefactor and beneficiary*' (Irani, 2018). People feel happier when their behaviour is motivated by others' well-being.

There are some simple ways to leverage the idea of helping others to help you find meaning.

You can start to do random acts of kindness (RAK) once a week at work: '*research evidence overwhelmingly confirms that RAK brings positive benefits to the individual giver, in terms of both mental and physical health gains*' (Passmore and Oades, 2015). Random acts of kindness are an important positive psychology intervention that involve doing a simple act of kindness for others that is unexpected to the receiver and motivated by compassion/kindness from the giver. Examples of RAKs include buying a coffee for a colleague, giving some unexpected positive feedback to someone, bringing in a treat for the team to share. Research shows to be most beneficial to happiness RAKs should be, as their name suggests, random (so not always the same act done at the same time) and not done every day (as they feel like a habit and lose their ability to make you feel happier). You could also find time to volunteer for good causes outside of work to help others. People who volunteer feel more satisfied with their lives and rate their health better compared to those who don't volunteer (Lawton et al, 2021).

Building on the idea that meaning is found through our connections to others, I love this idea from Steger, a positive psychologist, to create a meaning treasure trove. You can do this by taking photos of all the things that provide meaning in your life. This could be people (friends, colleagues, family), hobbies, music, books, films, places. You can then compile them into an electronic album or print them out as a physical album. You can look through your album of meaning when you are having a difficult day or when you need reminding of what is important for you.

The balance of your life

When I work with clients who are struggling to find meaning in their working lives, one way to support finding more meaning is to look at where they are focusing their energy. We then discuss whether they are comfortable with their focus, and what changes they would like to make to refocus their energy in other areas.

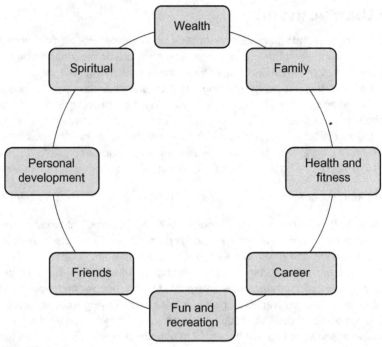

Figure 5.1 Life balance

Focus of energy exercise

This is based on the idea of the Wheel of Life, which is a circle that has different spokes of the wheel with each spoke representing a different aspect of your life. The original Wheel of Life was created by Paul Meyer in the 1960s as a coaching tool, and it has been used and adapted by many coaches since. This is an adaption of the Wheel of Life.

Look at the eight different areas of life in the diagram and decide which three you have put the most energy into recently (in the last three months)?

Now reflect on which are the three that you put the least energy into in the last three months.

- How comfortable are you with your top three and bottom three?
- Are there any areas you would like to give more energy to?
- Are there any areas you would like to give less energy to?
- What could you change to ensure you give your energy where you would like to?

Leadership and meaning

I want to feel like I make a difference.
I want to look back on my life and feel satisfied with my career.
I want to be able to see the impact of my work.
What is it all for?
Does it really matter?
No one listens to what is important to me.

These are some of the words you may hear from team members or colleagues when they are questioning their feeling of meaning or purpose at work.

Leaders can build meaningful workplaces by referring to the CARMA model (Steger, 2017). CARMA stands for:

- clarity – ensuring the team knows and believes in the vision;
- authenticity – acting ethically and honestly;
- respect – building positive relationships;
- mattering – conveying how important a worker's contribution is;
- autonomy – allowing people autonomy in their work.

Mattering

One of the components of the CARMA model that stands out to me is mattering. Mattering is simple – helping team members feel like they matter. This can be done in one-to-ones, ad hoc conversations, team meetings, performance reviews, over email, on Teams, in messages. Mattering involves reminding people how what they are doing links to the broader goals of the team and the business and celebrating when things go well – and looking to learn when things don't go well. Mattering helps with all four sources of meaning, as it builds self-worth, shows how people are effective and links individual purpose to a broader purpose. Mattering can also help the values source of meaning, as a leader can give positive feedback on seeing certain values in action, such as agility, authenticity and positivity – whatever has been seen, and also links to what the organisation values.

I recently facilitated a team building day and I saw the director speak to his team. They are a new team formed from the consolidation of two teams and face challenges of resources, training new team members, adjusting to working together as one, and cultural changes across the broader organisation. The director did a fantastic job of mattering by reminding the team that what they do is vital to the new direction of the organisation, and how their part in the future is critical. He reminded them how talented they are, and how they are in their roles because they are the right people to manage these changes successfully. He also told them he had their back, because they matter, and that if they faced challenges that they could not influence or control in their roles through dealings with other departments he would help and support and join them in the challenge.

By leaders telling people why they matter, this helps people feel like they do meaningful work. They feel acknowledged and heard, which feeds into our basic needs as humans to feel competent, have autonomy and feel part of something bigger than ourselves.

SUMMARY CHECKLIST

To increase meaning at work there are four needs to be satisfied:

1. purpose;
2. values;
3. self-worth;
4. efficacy.

Having more meaning at work increases well-being and performance. People are increasingly looking for greater meaning in their work.

You can increase you own meaning and others by doing some practical tasks such as:

- understanding your own values or your team members' values and reflecting on how they complement the values of the organisation;
- reflecting on where you are putting your energy in work and life and where you would like to make changes;
- focusing on how you can contribute to others outside of yourself – colleagues, the business, your community.
- understanding what makes your heart sing at work using the concept of *ikigai*;
- as a leader increasing '*mattering*' with your teams – help team members understand why they matter at work and how they contribute to the bigger picture.

REFLECTIONS

Having meaning at work is not dichotomous: you don't do meaningful work or not do meaningful work. Having meaning in your work is a spectrum with all shades of grey, and this can change from one day to the next. What you want to aim for is having more days that feel meaningful than days that don't. Everyone has to do tasks at work that they like doing less and hold less meaning. Everyone has days where they feel less purpose or lower self-esteem, or are doing work further from their values, and days where they feel less effective. That is the challenge of work and life, that life involves struggle, change and challenge.

I have been asked before if it is possible to have '*too much meaning*' in life or work, and what would that look like or mean. To answer this question, I look to transpersonal coaching (a type of coaching that aims to help clients find meaning). Transpersonal coaches explain that people who focus more on a life of meaning, and less on a life of traditional achievement – such as a higher paid job, or a job with more responsibilities – can have a crisis of duality, where they look to realign their life to not just live life for meaning but to also strive for achievement. This is the opposite of someone who has focused considerably on achievement, who may have a crisis of meaning when they reach middle age and ask, '*What is this all for?*'. So, yes, people can feel that they have prioritised meaning too much and that they want to realign the balance.

If there was just one insight that you could take for yourself or to help teams in regard to understanding meaning, and how to increase it at work, then I would say this: meaning can come from a transient moment that comes and goes in seconds, and meaning can come from looking to the future and connecting what you are working for now to what you will achieve through that work in the future. Both hold tremendous power. Finding meaning in the present is the trick often missed. You can feel meaning in making a team member smile, completing a project, having a great collaborative client conversation or celebrating an achievement at work. Meaning does not have to involve struggle or grand plans. Feeling that something has meaning can be simple, and it can be found in everyday conversations and situations all the time.

SELF-COACHING QUESTIONS

Work through GROW for this topic and do add more questions/reflections at each stage than are detailed here if you want to explore further.

Goal (to uncover what your aim is)

- What specifically would I like to improve with regard to:
  - my sense of meaning at work?
  - my team's sense of meaning at work?
  - the four sources of meaning for myself and/or my team: purpose, values, efficacy and self-worth?

Reality (to understand)

- What is going on for me that makes this something I would like to change?
- When have I had the most meaning in my work over my career? What made me have more meaning then?
- How aware am I of how my colleagues or team feel about how meaningful their work is?

Options (to explore)

- What could I do to increase meaning at work for myself and for my team?
- Who, apart from myself, needs to make a change in my team?
- What else might I do?
- If I woke up tomorrow and my goal had been reached, what would be the first thing I would notice that was different?

Will (to decide on action)

- What will I need to do now?
- What is the first step I will take and when?
- What deadlines will I set for myself?

REFERENCES

Achor, S, Reece, A, Kellerman, G R and Robichaux, A (2018) 9 Out of 10 People Are Willing to Earn Less Money to Do More-Meaningful Work. *Harvard Business Review*. [online] Available at: https://hbr.org/2018/11/9-out-of-10-people-are-willing-to-earn-less-money-to-do-more-meaningful-work (accessed 7 March 2023).

Ackerman, C E (2018) What Is Self-worth and How Do We Build It? PositivePsychology.com. [online] Available at: https://positivepsychology.com/self-worth/ (accessed 8 March 2023).

Allan, B A et al (2018) Outcomes of Meaningful Work: A Meta-Analysis. *Journal of Management Studies*, 56(3). doi: 10.1111/joms.12406.

Bailey, C, Yoeman, R, Madden, A, Thompson, M and Kerridge, G (2019) A Review of the Empirical Literature on Meaningful Work: Progress and Research Agenda. *Human Resource Development Review*, 18(1): 83–113.

Baumeister, R F and Vohs, K D (2001) The Pursuit of Meaningfulness in Life. In Lopez, S J and Snyder, C R (eds) *The Handbook of Positive Psychology* (ch. 44, p 608). Oxford: Oxford University Press.

Cambridge Dictionary (nd) Self-worth. [online] Available at: https://dictionary.cambridge.org/dictionary/english/self-worth (accessed 3 April 2023).

Duncan, R D (2018) The Why of Work: Purpose and Meaning Really Do Matter. [online] Available at: www.forbes.com/sites/rodgerdeanduncan/2018/09/11/the-why-of-work-purpose-and-meaning-really-do-matter/?sh=4df1300868e1 (accessed 8 March 2023).

Frankl, V E (2004) *Man's Search for Meaning.* London: Penguin Random House.

Garcia, H and Miralles, F (2017) *Ikigai: The Japanese Secret to a Long and Happy Life.* London: Hutchinson.

Irani, A S (2018) Positive Altruism: Helping that Benefits Both the Recipient and Giver. Master of Applied Positive Psychology (MAPP) Capstone Projects. 152. [online] Available at: https://repository.upenn.edu/mapp_capstone/152/ (accessed 8 March 2023).

Lawton, R N, Gramatki, I, Watt, W and Fujiwara, D (2021) Does Volunteering Make Us Happier, or Are Happier People More Likely to Volunteer? Addressing the Problem of Reverse Causality When Estimating the Wellbeing Impacts of Volunteering. *Journal of Happiness Studies*, 22: 599–624. doi: 10.1007/s10902-020-00242-8.

McKinsey Quarterly (2020) Purpose: Shifting From Why to How. [online] Available at: www.mckinsey.com/capabilities/people-and-organizational-performance/our-insights/purpose-shifting-from-why-to-how#/ (accessed 3 April 2023).

Passmore, J and Oades, L G (2015) Positive Psychology Coaching Techniques: Random Acts of Kindness, Consistent Acts of Kindness and Empathy. *The Coaching Psychologist*, 11(2): 90–2.

Steger, M (2017) Creating Meaning and Purpose at Work. In Oades, L G, Steger, M F, Delle Fave, A and Passmore, A (eds) *The Wiley Blackwell Handbook of the Psychology of Positivity and Strengths-Based Approaches at Work*. doi: 10.1002/ 9781118977620.ch5.

Steger, M F (2018) Meaning and Well-being. In Diener, E, Oishi, S and Tay, L (eds) *Handbook of Well-being*. Salt Lake City, UT: DEF Publishers.

Towers Perrin (2012) Employee Engagement Global Workforce Study. [online] Available at: https://employe eengagement.com/towers-perrin-employee-engagement/ (accessed 8 March 2023).

Van Wingerden, J and Van der Stoep, J (2018) The Motivational Potential of Meaningful Work: Relationships with Strengths Use, Work Engagement, and Performance. *PLoS ONE*, 13(6): e0197599. doi: 10.1371/journal.pone.0197599.

6

Accomplishment

A sense of accomplishment is a result of working toward and reaching goals, mastering an endeavour, and having self-motivation to finish what you set out to do.

(Seligman, 2002)

The final element of PERMA is the A that stands for accomplishment or achievement. In this chapter we will explore how having a sense of accomplishment/achievement helps performance and well-being at work, and how it links with the other elements of PERMA. The important words in the previous sentence are '*sense of*'. This chapter is not about what to achieve, or how high to aim, but how to feel like you are achieving and the massive impact the sense of accomplishment has on your well-being and future performance. It is also about having a sense that you *can* achieve, that you can set goals and work towards them.

HOPE THEORY

One of the ideas from positive psychology relevant to feeling a sense of accomplishment is Hope theory. Not only is it useful to look back on something and feel good that you achieved it, it is also vital to look ahead and feel a strong sense of agency and hope that you will be able to accomplish what you would like to. '*Hope*' (like compassion) is not a word that is used much in the workplace in relation to performance. When someone '*hopes*' it will go well, it tends to imply a non-specific hunch that things might work out, or if someone is relying on '*hope*' it suggests they are not relying on their own hard work, preparation or evidence. However, '*hope*' is not the same as wishing or dreaming. Hope theory proposes that having '*hope*' is vastly underestimated when it comes to predicting whether someone will perform well and achieve their goals. Hope is a powerful human strength that should be recognised and cultivated in the workplace.

Goals

Positive psychologists say Hope theory describes how people move positively towards their goals. Having hope is described as a positive motivational state that is enabled by goals, pathways to reach goals and agency (the feeling of control over actions and their consequences) (Snyder, 2002). Hope is different to optimism as optimists may believe everything will work out, but don't necessarily have the motivation to act to make good things happen, might not have goals or have thought through how to overcome barriers. Conversely, high hopers have clear, valuable goals. The relationship between goals and achievement has been well documented. Having goals is strongly linked to being more self-motivated and driven (Locke and Latham, 2006). Goals help us by enlightening us – giving us an insight into our desires, strengths, weaknesses and vision for the future. They also encourage us as writing out a goal gives us motivation, especially if we let others know about it, and goals enable us, as they give us confidence to reach into the future with positivity. It is useful to understand the two different types of goals – those that are extrinsically motivating, and those that are intrinsically motivating. In Chapter 3 on strengths I introduced the idea of intrinsic and extrinsic motivation – when we are intrinsically motivated to do something this means we do it for the enjoyment and growth it brings us rather than an external reward or recognition, such as money or status. We need a balance of the two types of goal in our lives that we are intrinsically and extrinsically motivated to work towards.

Pathways

High hopers also have an ability to develop a number of specific pathways that can lead to the goal. Developing pathways is about working out how you can move from where you are now to where you would like to be and having a number of routes that could get you there. When you have already thought through different pathways, when setbacks happen, or circumstances change, then those who have thought through different routes are far more likely to persevere to achieve the goal. The other routes are not inferior pathways, but alternative pathways that ensure you won't fail.

High hopers have a willingness to initiate and maintain motivation to follow the pathways and be flexible in which pathway to follow. This helps people to have strategies to overcome barriers, have a will to succeed and a belief that success will come from determination, effort and energy. With my clients in coaching there have been many times when people have come to me feeling hopeless – that their route to success is unclear or blocked, and through discussing the situation they have realised that there are routes to their vision and they have a new way forward. I was recently working with a coachee who wanted to identify a 'Plan B' career path. 'Plan A' was likely to not be possible due to the coachee's health situation. He was extremely unhappy about possibly not being able to follow his Plan A. While it was extremely helpful for him to explore another career option, we talked about the impact of the language he was using. For him, 'Plan B' meant an inferior option. When he tried substituting 'Plan B' for 'An alternative career path', this helped him to see another option as not necessarily inferior, just different, and as such increased his interest and motivation in being able to explore other pathways – his hope increased.

Agency

When people who have high hope meet barriers or problems, they react differently to those who have low hope. Those with high hope view barriers as challenges that they will work to overcome, and they see different pathways to meet their goal. Those with low hope are more likely to feel defeated, give up or change their goal to a lesser outcome. They are also more likely to attempt to bring others down with them. When I am working with a client who has low hope in achieving their coaching goals, the very first thing we will work on is their level of belief, hope and motivation to achieve the goal, and to be able to do that in an environment that could be constantly changing. Complexity means there nearly always needs to be a number of pathways. Sometimes a client can be set on one pathway, and one pathway alone, and is not willing to entertain other pathways. It is then useful to help the client understand what is wedding them to that idea alone, and what will they do if they have setbacks. All of these combine: goals, pathways and agency to enable action, which sets Hope theory apart from theories of self-efficacy and motivation. Having high hope does have strong parallels with having a growth mindset, versus a fixed mindset. As Dweck, who coined the term growth mindset. says: *'In the fixed mindset, everything is about the outcome. If you fail – or if you're the best – it's all been wasted. The growth mindset allows people to value what they're doing regardless of the outcome'* (Dweck, 2017).

Table 6.1 Hope theory (Snyder, 2002)

Clear valuable goals
Number of specific pathways to the goal
Agency: Motivation and flexibility to get started and overcome barriers

As a leader, if you want to cultivate hope in your people, setting them goals or empowering them to set clear goals is not enough. People also need to have the freedom to explore and follow a number of pathways to get to the goal, and motivation to start work, and overcome problems.

I love this quote from Charles Snyder, the founding psychologist of Hope theory, who said, *'A rainbow is a prism that sends shards of multi-coloured light in various directions. It lifts our spirits and makes us think of what is possible. Hope is the same – a personal rainbow of the mind'* (Snyder, 2002).

If someone has a goal but does not reach it or sets impossibly high goals and then sacrifices everything to reach it, this can be damaging to physical and mental health. Many high achievers that I have worked with over the years have shown me that it is often the most ambitious and talented people who push themselves towards their goals in all areas of their life to then suffer symptoms of stress and even burnout. What can we learn from Hope theory to help people who tend towards over-working and achieving goals at all costs? Hope theory underlines the importance of a number of pathways to achieve a goal. High achievers who end up burnt out often become narrowly focused, blurring out their peripheral vision because it is painful to see the impact on themselves (and sometimes others) of their single-minded determination to get where they need to get to.

Avoiding burnout should involve not only being *aware* of triggers, signs and symptoms of feeling overstretched, but importantly *doing* something differently at that point. If you have high hope (in the context of Hope theory) you will find it much easier to recognise that the pathway you are on is not the only pathway – as you will already have thought of a number of pathways. The signs of stress and a lowering of mental health are warnings that you need to find an alternative pathway and hope will enable you to do that, not reluctantly, but optimistically and positively. The goals may even need to move, but someone with high hope will see that that is OK, and is a strategic move in itself, not a disappointment or failure.

ACCOMPLISHMENT, PERFORMANCE AND WELL-BEING

Personal accomplishment – the small things we achieve each day, and the larger projects or milestones we achieve – help build our sense of self efficacy and self-esteem. This is a continuous feedback loop as the more we feel we accomplish, the more we feel we are able to accomplish. What can be tricky for people is realising what exactly they have accomplished and being able to pause and feel pride and triumph in that accomplishment. Often people can be too busy or too self-critical to acknowledge achievements and use the motivation from that achievement to continue to grow and learn. Wanting to accomplish and feeling a sense of accomplishment are both linked to higher performance at work and feelings of wellness and happiness.

Having goals to achieve enables high performance in four different ways. Goals direct energy and attention towards the goal and away from other activities that might take energy and time away, they give energy, especially if the goals are stretching enough, without being too ambitious or unachievable. Goals also increase persistence and focus – aptly illustrated by anyone who has worked far longer and with more concentration when a tight deadline is ahead (Locke and Latham, 2002).

Seeking to reach goals and having a sense of accomplishment are also linked to higher well-being. The reasons for this are linked firmly to other topics we have covered in the P, E and M of PERMA. Having intrinsic goals that are in line with our values increase our feelings of purpose and meaning. Research shows that intrinsic life goals mean greater happiness and satisfaction with life, compared with extrinsic life goals (Deci et al, 1999; Niemiec et al, 2009). Having goals that are based on our strengths and interests increases motivation, positive emotions and the chances of accomplishing and feeling self-efficacious. Maslow's theory of motivation explains how intrinsic goals satisfy one of our fundamental human needs. Maslow proposed that we have a hierarchy of needs as humans: basic needs such as food, water, shelter, and the feeling of being safe. Once these are satisfied we have psychological needs, such as the need for belonging and accomplishment. At the top of the hierarchy of needs is the desire for self-actualisation – being able to fulfil our full potential. The A of PERMA is about satisfying the psychological need of accomplishment, and the self-fulfilment need of reaching potential with intrinsic goals.

ENABLING A SENSE OF ACCOMPLISHMENT

Now let's consider some practical ideas and tools that we can apply at work to enable motivation and a sense of accomplishment to improve performance and well-being.

Have clear, positive goals

The thinking that goes into formulating the goal is just as important as the thinking that goes into achieving the goal. If the goal is inadequate or not fully thought through, then it can be incredibly hard to achieve. Not putting time into getting the goal right is like entering a race and not knowing where the finish line is.

Much has been written about goal setting in the workplace, with SMART goals being suggested as the most effective type. These are:

- **s**pecific – detailed enough that you know exactly what you are aiming for;
- **m**easurable – you know when you have achieved success;
- **a**chievable – within reach;
- **r**elevant – appropriate and helpful to your current position in life or work;
- **t**imely – setting a time by which you will achieve the goal.

Setting goals using SMART can be very effective. However, using SMART to structure goals has two drawbacks. The first drawback is that it emphasises setting a goal that is achievable, which can make you set a more conservative goal than perhaps you are capable of, or would really like to dare to dream of. Second, it misses out some key elements that I have found really bring goals to life: owning the goal, a '*towards*' goal, and a goal that can have different stages or be adapted. I prefer using my own acronym, MAPS. MAPS goals are:

- **M**ine – something you buy into, or you set, not something imposed on you;
- **A**mbitious – bold enough that it will make a difference;
- **P**ositive – framed in a way that you are seeking more of something, not less, that you are working towards something, not away from something;
- **S**pecific but **S**tepped – something that has a clear direction and is not fuzzy or undefined, but can change depending upon circumstances.

Mine

If we are involved in formulating our own targets and goals we are more likely to be accountable to meet those targets as we understand more about them and why the target or goal is useful – the 'why' of the goal. As we looked at in the chapter on engagement, one of the basic needs for enabling intrinsic motivation is autonomy. Being involved in goal-setting increases autonomy and can therefore increase motivation. Imposed goals are those that your manager might set you at work without discussion or consultation. '*If the goal is assigned tersely (e.g., "Do this...") without explanation, it leads to performance that is significantly lower than for a participatively set goal*' (Locke and Latham, 2002).

Ryan and Deci (2000), psychologists who developed the theory of self-determination, say: '*Comparisons between people whose motivation is authentic (literally, self-authored or endorsed) and those who are merely externally controlled for an action typically reveal that the former, relative to the latter, have more interest, excitement, and confidence, which in turn is manifest both as enhanced performance, persistence, and creativity*'.

Therefore, if managers, allow their team members to participate in goal-setting and mutually agree their goals (within the remit of the organisational or departmental purpose) this can increase motivation and performance.

Ambitious

A recent analysis that spanned 30 years of studies on self-regulated learning found that the level of goal set (easy to achieve through to hard to achieve) correlated strongly with the level of learning that actually took place. Therefore, the higher the goal set, the higher the learning was in the end (Sitzmann and Ely, 2011). Thirty-five years of research on goal setting by Locke and Latham (2002) also showed clearly that ambitious goals are energising and lead to greater effort than low goals.

Positive

It is also important that goals are framed in a positive *'towards'* light – that they are looking for more of something, not less, they are moving towards something, not away from something. Therefore, less effective goals would be to *'reduce stress in the workplace'*, or *'decrease absenteeism'*, or *'decrease conflict conversations'*.

> *'I want to be less stressed' … 'I want to stop losing my temper' … 'I want my team to have less anxiety' … 'I want my organisation to be less pressurised'.*

All of these are goals involve having less of something. They are called avoidance goals.

When the goal you want to achieve involves having *'less'* it can be far more difficult to achieve and far less intrinsically motivating than a goal that wants more. Avoidance goals have been shown to be associated with less satisfaction with progress, less satisfaction with competence to achieve the goal, and even less satisfaction with life (Elliot and Church, 1997).

Instead, it is far more helpful to ask yourself what you want more of instead, which is an approach-orientated goal. If you want to be less stressed, then what do you want more of instead? To be calmer? To be enthusiastic? If you want to stop being nervous when you are presenting to a group, then how *do* you want to feel when you present to a group? Confident? At ease, perhaps? By asking yourself what you want more of instead it helps you to understand what it is exactly that you *do* want instead, and you can start to put a plan in place to reach it.

If you think about celebrating and being motivated by reaching your goals then it is much easier to celebrate and be motivated by more-type goals. A less goal: *'I have reached the level of stress that I was aiming for – really low!'* Or a more goal: *'I have become so much calmer and happier since making X changes to my working day'.* These *'more'* goals are also called approach goals. A common lifestyle goal – especially in January – is *'to lose weight'.* This is an avoidance goal. A more helpful goal that would result in the same endpoint but is much more positive and motivational is an approach goal such as *'to increase daily walking to build up to doing a 2k walk every day of the week'.*

'More' type goals are much more *'sticky'.* You remember them, you can have a more concrete plan to reach them, and you know far more clearly when you have reached them. Sticky goals are what you are looking for. To turn a negative *'less'* goal into a positive approach goal, you can ask yourself:

> *And when I XXXX [negative/less outcome, such as 'when I am less stressed'] has been achieved then what happens?*

If the answer is still negative or a '*less than*' answer, then ask the question again. Ask '*And then what happens next?*' until you reach a positive towards goal.

Sometimes we cannot even see past the problem to even get to a '*less goal*'. For example, we might be stuck on '*I am just too stressed when presenting to senior managers*'. This is a problem, not a goal. To move from a problem to a goal, ask yourself '*When "problem" what would I like to have happen?*' For example, '*When I'm too nervous presenting what would I like to happen?*' The answer might be to be less nervous.

Then, as before ask: '*When I am less nervous* then what happens?'

Possible answers could be: '*I am more confident*', '*I get my message across more clearly*'. These are great '*more-type*' goals.

Specific and stepped

A specific and stepped goal can set the right route to achieve the goal, otherwise you can end up being busy without actually moving towards where you want to get to. The best way to explain this is to imagine a car journey where you are entering a postcode into the sat-nav. If you have the exact postcode, then the car will follow the most direct route to get there. But it may be that you want to take a longer route in the car to see the view, or collect something, or someone, or stop off along the way to rethink your plan. A stepped goal means you can reflect at different stages, change things as you move forward and be flexible to respond to your current, changing environment, a relevant concern in the modern, fast-changing working environment. Rigidity of goals can be restricting and demotivating – this is especially the case if it is a longer-term goal. Have you ever worked towards something, and then when you have got there wondered why you wanted to get there in the first place?

Positive feedback

People are usually quite good at giving themselves feedback when the feedback is negative. Negative self-talk such as '*I didn't do that well*'; '*That could have been better*'; '*I didn't land my point at all well*'. '*I should have prepared more*' is quite common. What people are usually far less good at is giving themselves positive feedback. I find it interesting that there are many double-barrelled words that begin with self such: as '*self-esteem*', '*self-belief*' and '*self-validation*' which have positive meanings. What positive word sums up giving yourself positive feedback? Being self-congratulatory is an option. Yet the definition of self-congratulatory is '*unduly complacent or proud regarding one's personal achievements or qualities; self-satisfied*' (Oxford Languages Dictionary). Self-praising might also fit the brief. The definition for this is '*the action of praising oneself; boasting*' (Oxford Language Dictionary). Therefore, the meaning of being self-congratulatory or self-praising is being complacent, self-satisfied or boastful. Who would want to be those things? In the workplace the focus is often on development, weaknesses, feedback to improve, what didn't work, with far less positive feedback, encouragement and triumph. No wonder we aren't good at giving ourselves positive feedback.

TOP TIPS FOR POSITIVE SELF-FEEDBACK

- Allow time to self-reflect after milestones are reached or goals achieved and ask yourself: What went well and how did I help to make that happen?
- Ask colleagues, stakeholders and managers for positive feedback, and say that you want to know because you want to do more of what works.
- Write down three positive things that you have done each week, and keep this as a sunshine diary of positive actions or events. Refer to it during a tough week. Learn from it to see if there are patterns, share ideas with other colleagues of what worked. You can also do this for your team, then feedback three positive things you have seen in the team.
- Ask yourself what strengths you used when you have overcome a problem and reflect how you might use those strengths in future difficult situations.
- Give yourself specific feedback when something has gone well, use the format AID.
  - **A**ction – what was the action you did?
  - **I**mpact – what impact did that have?
  - **D** – what will you **d**o now knowing this? (Do more, do again, do more frequently.)

Giving positive feedback to others in your team or business enables a sense of accomplishment in others. You can use the AID structure on giving yourself positive feedback with others (Action, Impact, Do).

Appreciation and recognition are two different things. Recognition is giving positive feedback to someone on something they have done well or achieved. The feedback is based on their performance on a task or project. Appreciation is giving feedback on the value of the person, regardless of achievements. The feedback is based on the qualities they have. For example, you could give feedback to someone in your team on how much you value a particular strength they have, or how much you value the support they gave you or others during a tough period. You are recognising the person not for what they achieved but for what they bring to the team. When businesses recruit they often interview based on looking for what the person can bring – the qualities the person has, as well as the experience, that will benefit and fit with the team. This focus on qualities and fit can be continued, as the person still has those qualities (and hopefully shows them).

Leaders may feel hesitancy to give appreciation feedback as they may feel more comfortable giving feedback on an outcome rather than on a quality such as a strength. Giving appreciation can still be specific, though, and about something you can see and give examples of, not something intangible. For example, if showing appreciation for a strength, you could say: '*I noticed that you have really stayed optimistic during difficult times in the last year, for example, always focusing on the things we have achieved, not what we haven't, and talking about challenges not problems, and that strength has really helped the team to stay motivated.*'

SOLUTION-FOCUSED COACHING (SFC)

To enable a sense of accomplishment and to encourage and motivate yourself and others, you can use solution-focused coaching. SFC is a type of coaching that focuses on solutions and does not dwell on problems. SFC is massively complementary to the ideas from positive psychology, as the underpinning focus of positive psychology is to focus on what works, and what is good, rather than what doesn't work. Solution-focused coaching reframes problems as challenges to be overcome.

SFC is about clarifying goals, highlighting resources that you have available to reach those goals, and thinking about the future and what future success looks like. There are some simple but powerful tools from SFC that you can use for yourself and with others. The first step in SFC is to clarify for yourself or with the person you are supporting, what is the goal of the conversation. This needs to be a positive, towards goal, as we discussed earlier in this chapter. Once the goal is established you can use some of the other SFC tools that help people think and move them towards the solution.

SFC is especially useful when you or others feel low on confidence or motivation to make a change. One tool in SFC aims to help you recall a previous situation when things have gone well, and how you can translate that experience to a situation where things are not going so well. This is exception-hunting. The approach has its roots in therapy; in the 1980s therapists working in a family therapy centre had become disillusioned with an approach that focused on the problem and finding root causes. They began to ask questions that focused clients on solutions instead. Research has shown the method to be very effective in personal and workplace coaching (Green, 2006). This approach asks you to think with a solutions emphasis, rather than a problems emphasis.

The best way to illustrate this is to use an example. Imagine that your goal is to improve your relationship at work with a particular person or group of people. A solution-focused approach asks you to think about people you *do* have good relationships with, and what you do or feel differently with those people versus those you do not. For example, you may ask one of these questions.

- Who at work do you have good relationships with, who is most similar in position or character to the person/people you are aiming to improve your relationship with?
- Describe what it is that makes you have a good relationship with that person/people. What do you do differently with them?
- How are you different with them?

You can also reflect on whether there have ever been any moments when the relationship *has* been better.

- Have you ever had a moment of really great rapport with the person/people you are aiming to improve your relationship with? What made that moment different to all others?

Another example could be, if your goal was to improve your presentations to senior people, your reflections would focus on what presentations you have done that have gone well, and what was different about them, or whether there is a group of people who you present to and find it much easier. You can explore what is different about presenting to that easier group. You would also look to uncover what does go well when you present to senior people. You are hunting out the good in the whole situation – your strengths, your resources and your competencies in relation to your goal.

You can explore the following in relation to the goal.

- What does go well/works?
- What has worked before/has gone well before?
- What strengths do you bring to this?
- What resources do you have to support you?
- Who you know who does do this well? What do they do?

A so-called '*miracle question*' is also part of the solution-focused coaching. The question was developed by Steve de Shazer – he was one of the pioneers of the solution-focused approach (Bannick, 2007).

The question is:

> *Suppose that one night, while you are asleep, there is a miracle and the problem that brought you here is solved. However, because you are asleep you don't know that the miracle has already happened. When you wake up in the morning, what will be different that will tell you that the miracle has taken place? What else?*

The action is to imagine waking up in the morning and a magical, miracle happening has occurred, and your problem is solved, or your outcome is achieved. You ask yourself, what is the first thing you would notice as you go about your day that your problem had been solved, and how would the day progress? These questions help you focus on the desired future. They also help you pinpoint what it is that really will be different when the desired future is realised. For example, it may be that your desired outcome is to improve your relationship with your manager. Your explanation of your morning might be that as soon as you wake up things are different, as you feel calm going into work. You can also ask yourself, what is the first thing that others would notice to know that the miracle had taken place?

A variation of the question is to ask yourself to imagine your desired future and see yourself as you want to be. Then to work back from that, asking yourself what you need to do at each step to get there.

Another SFC tool is asking a scaling question such as: how confident are you out of 10 [to do X] where 10 is supremely confident, and 1 is not confident at all? (X could be presenting to the board, leading the team to success on the project, increasing staff retention, increasing turnover, or whatever the topic is you are working on.) You would then ask yourself, or the person you are supporting: what makes it this number and not lower? You can then ask, where would I like to be on the ladder? And what do I need to do to be an '*X*'? This will identify what you need to do to move forward. You can also substitute '*confident*' for '*committed*'. For example: how committed are you to X on a scale of 1–10, where 10 is completely committed. The exercise works if you focus on the actions the individual can take, rather than reflecting on things that could happen to someone or things other people could do that might impact on where you are on the ladder.

INDIVIDUAL PPI

Self-coaching exercise using a solution-focused approach

- Choose a change you would like to make and articulate this as a positive goal.
- Now ask yourself out of 10 how confident are you that you can reach that goal?
- What makes you choose that number not lower?
- Where would you like to be on the ladder?
- What needs to happen for you to move up?

SUMMARY CHECKLIST

- Hope theory explains how people can move positively towards their goals.
- Having clear, positive goals enables high performance.
- Defining a number of pathways to achieve a goal is associated with feeling motivated and with achieving the goal.
- People with high hope view barriers as challenges to be overcome.
- Personal accomplishments build self-efficacy and self-esteem.
- Being able to give yourself positive feedback is a useful life skill.
- Solution-focused coaching is a useful skill to enable a sense of accomplishment in yourself and others.

REFLECTIONS

A really common anxiety in the workplace and in life is '*Am I doing OK?*' I have lost count of the number of times senior leaders I work with say that they have a sense of anxiety about their own performance or ability which can impact on well-being. In some cases, this is such an entrenched repeated pattern of thought it is known as imposter syndrome. Imposter syndrome is the chronic feeling of being inadequate despite apparent success, usually combined with a feeling that you may be '*found out*' at any moment for being inadequate, that you are a fraud. There is a distinction between imposter syndrome that can show repeatedly throughout someone's career – the entrenched chronic pattern of thought – and fleeting feelings of inadequacy or feeling '*out of your depth*' in certain situations.

I have known people who have imposter syndrome and people who have fleeting or periodic feelings of inadequacy. I have witnessed one element they both have in common – the relationship the person has with their accomplishments. When people feel like a fraud either fleetingly or chronically, in the times of self-doubt they do not have an easy relationship with their accomplishments, they do not feel the sense of pride and achievement that others without self-doubt might feel. Even having accomplished great personal achievements, people can look at their achievements and think: '*I achieved a great success, but underneath I have no idea how I did it, and I could be found out for that.*' The sense of accomplishment is tainted with a sense of fraudulent success.

Therefore, the ideas in this chapter from positive psychology can help people who have self-doubt. A *sense* of achievement or accomplishment is far more impactful on people's motivation and confidence than any particular achievement that I could describe here. With a sense of accomplishment, there has to come pride, satisfaction and a recognition of personal ability. Therefore, developing a feeling of pride and happiness in your achievements can help protect you from feelings of insecurity, low self-esteem and self-doubt. If you can be proud of yourself and enable pride in others, imagine how powerful that is to transform your own and others' performance at work.

SELF-COACHING QUESTIONS

Work through GROW for this topic and do add more questions/reflections at each stage than are detailed here if you want to explore further.

Goal (to uncover what your aim is)

- What specifically would I like to improve with regards to:
  - my sense of accomplishment?
  - my team's sense of accomplishment?
  - my motivation to achieve?
  - my team's motivation to achieve?

Reality (to understand)

- What is going on for me or my team that makes this something I would like to change?
- How much of a sense of accomplishment do I usually feel in my working day?
- What have I done recently that has given me a sense of accomplishment?
- What has my team done recently that has given them a sense of accomplishment?

Options (to explore)

- What could I do to increase my sense of accomplishment at work for myself and for my team?
- Who, apart from myself, needs to make a change in my team?
- If I woke up tomorrow and my goal had been reached, what would be the first thing I would notice that was different?

Will (to decide on action)

- What actions will I take?
- What is the first step I will take and when?
- What deadlines will I set for myself?

REFERENCES

Bannick, F P (2007) Solution Focused Brief Therapy. *Journal of Contemporary Psychotherapy*, 37: 87–94.

Deci, E L, Koestner, R and Ryan, R M (1999) A Meta-analytic Review of Experiments Examining the Effects of Extrinsic Rewards on Intrinsic Motivation. *Psychological Bulletin*, 125(6): 627–68. doi: 10.1037/0033-2909.125.6.627.

Dweck, C (2017) *Mindset.* New York: Random House.

Elliot, A J and Church, M A (1997) A Hierarchical Model of Approach and Avoidance Achievement Motivation. *Journal of Personality and Social Psychology*, 72(1): 218–32. doi: 10.1037/0022-3514.72.1.218.

Green, J and Grant, A M (2006) *Solution-focused Coaching: Managing People in a Complex World.* London: Chartered Institute of Personal Development.

Locke, E A and Latham, G P (2002) Building a Practically Useful Theory of Goal Setting and Task Motivation: A 35-Year Odyssey. *American Psychologist*, 57(9): 705–17. doi: 10.1037/0003-066X.57.9.705

Locke, E A and Latham, G P (2006) New Directions in Goal-Setting Theory. *Current Directions in Psychological Science*, 15(5): 265–8. doi: 10.1111/j.1467-8721.2006.00449.x

Niemiec, C P, Ryan, R M and Deci, E L (2009) The Path Taken: Consequences of Attaining Intrinsic and Extrinsic Aspirations in Post-College Life. *Journal of Research in Personality*, 43: 291–306.

Ryan, R M and Deci, E L (2000) Self-determination Theory and the Facilitation of Intrinsic Motivation, Social Development and Well-Being. *American Psychologist*, 55(1): 68–78.

Seligman, M E P (2002) *Authentic Happiness.* London: Nicholas Brealey Publishing.

Sitzmann, T and Ely, K (2011) A Meta-analysis of Self-regulated Learning in Work-related Training and Educational Attainment: What We Know and Where We Need to Go. *Psychological Bulletin*, 137(3): 421–42. doi: 10.1037/a0022777.

Snyder, C R (2002) Hope Theory Rainbows in the Mind. *Psychological Inquiry*, 13(4): 249–75.

7 Resilience

A resilient person is one who is able to navigate towards the resources that they need to cope in difficult situations, as well as one who can negotiate to get these resources in a way that makes sense to them.

(Ungar, 2019a)

All of the elements of PERMA, the P, E, R, M and A, help build resilience. In this chapter we are going to particularly focus on resilience as a topic on its own as the ideas from positive psychology (in addition to PERMA) really help resilience in the workplace. Resilience is not the absence of stress or difficult times; it is the ability to manage times of change and challenge, which we all face in our personal and professional lives. The Chartered Institute of Professional Development define resilience as '*helping employees adapt, cope, gain resources, and respond positively to stressors in the workplace*' (CIPD, 2022).

Being resilient is something that you can actively do, not a quality that you have or do not have, and therefore resilience is a trait you can develop and a state you can encourage. Resilience means you can bounce back, you can return to where you were before a difficult challenge; this is called *recovery*. Or resilience can mean you adapt to a new change or challenge, which is *positive adaption*. Resilience can also mean you transform, where the challenge you face and the way that you manage the challenge leads to a *transformation*. A transformation is a dramatic or fundamental change.

Resilience lives within people, but people do not exist in isolation. People are connected to others, through families, friendships, workplaces and communities. While what goes on in a person's mind and heart is crucial to their resilience, resilience is also about the environment and the resources people have. It is a web of interactions between the individual and their environment that can enable recovery, positive adaption or transformation. Resilience is therefore not just mindset – a feeling of positivity, optimism and hope. Resilience is not only what is going on in your mind, it's also what you do to seek the resources you need to manage the change or challenge. Resilience is enabled by what we have and what we think (Ungar, 2019b). Ungar, a leading researcher from the positive psychology field on resilience, says: '*Resilience is not a DIY endeavour – it's a dance with the world. What I began to understand from my research is that when people actively put themselves into situations that brought out their best (in other words, when they changed the world around them), it triggered a cascade of individual transformations*' (Ungar, 2019a).

PERMA AND RESILIENCE

The CIPD report on resilience that summarises all the scientific evidence on workplace resilience concludes there are five areas that are most important in determining someone's resilience at work (CIPD, 2021). All five of them relate back to topics we have looked at from the PERMA model.

Table 7.1 PERMA and resilience model

Resilience factor	Explanation of resilience factor	Area of PERMA it relates to
Self-efficacy	Confidence in ability to accomplish a task or achieve a goal	A – achievement M – meaning
Positivity	Experiencing positive moods, eg joy, cheerfulness, enthusiasm and alertness	P – positive emotions
Sense of coherence	Believing that what happens in life is comprehensible, manageable and meaningful	A – achievement M – meaning
Social support	Support available from supervisors, co-workers, family and friends	R – relationships
Leader-member exchange	Positive interpersonal relations	E – engagement R – relationships

This shows how understanding positive psychology and doing actions in each of the areas of PERMA really supports individuals' and teams' resilience, which has significant impact on performance and well-being.

RESILIENCE, WORKPLACE PERFORMANCE AND WELL-BEING

There is a strong correlation between resilience in the workplace and job performance (Krush et al, 2013; Luthans et al, 2007). A recent review of a number of resilience workplace studies showed that resilience training at work improved personal resilience, well-being, mental health and performance (CIPD, 2021).

How does resilience help people at work perform better? Researchers suggest that resilient people deal better with adversity, experience more positive emotions (which gives people all the benefits we spoke of in Chapter 2) and are more flexible in response to change. All of this leads to improved engagement (which gives people all the benefits we spoke of in Chapter 3), and therefore improved performance.

The CIPD (2021) say that 'People managers and colleagues play critical roles in influencing how resilient employees are.' They also say: 'To the manager who tells an employee *they simply need to be more resilient, a fair response would be that their behaviour affects the employee's resilience.'* To help resilience in your teams, it is not just about helping people to have a resilient mindset, it is also about considering and moderating the environment within which they work to support their ability to be resilient and their ability to have the resources they need to be resilient. A key model in the psychology of work is the job demands-resources model (Bakker and Demerouti, 2007). This model proposes that the demands people have at work such as the physical, psychological and social demands, need to be matched with the resources of the job, and those resources include the support they receive from colleagues, managers and their teams. The authors of the model propose that people have their own personal resources that they bring (such as optimism, hope), in positive psychology terms, these are the strengths people bring to work, but also people need external resources that are provided in the workplace. It is the combination of the two types of resources that enable someone to be resilient and thrive.

There is also a clear evidenced link between resilience in the workplace and well-being at work. Multiple studies have shown that resilience has a protective effect for people for anxiety, burnout and depression. Resilience has also been shown to enhance life satisfaction and positive feelings/thoughts (Hu et al, 2015; Lee et al, 2013). Resilience also has a protective effect against stress felt from job pressure, conflicts at work, bullying and job insecurity.

RESILIENT TEAMS

What is *'team resilience'*? The definition is very similar to individual resilience in that it is about being able to cope through adversity, but it also includes the emphasis on coming together to manage changes and challenges. If you have a group of individuals who are separately very resilient people, would they make a resilient team? Not necessarily.

'A team of resilient members may not necessarily demonstrate high resilience as the group interaction may still be characterised by a lack of communication or support, which can result in poor management of disruptions' (Alliger et al, 2015). It is how the team comes together that matters, and how the leader aligns people behind the team's common goals. A resilient team can enable resiliency in lesser resilient members of the team; a resilient leader can enable resiliency in all of their team members. In this way, resiliency can be catching, just as positivity can be.

So, what makes a resilient team? Recent studies have shown that to enable resilience in a team key elements are: a strong team identity, shared mental models, cohesion and trust between team members, and strong psychological safety (Sharma and Sharma, 2016). When team members have these in place they are better equipped to deal with adversity and change, and they will communicate better, increasingly cooperate more and support each other more comprehensively.

The extent of a team's resilience is clearly demonstrated in what happens to a team after a difficult or stressful time. A resilient team will persist, recover and/or show growth. A less resilient team will falter, lose team members (high attrition), suffer lower performance and lower well-being.

As a leader in the in the workplace, enabling resilient teams is about helping individuals to have a conducive environment for them to prepare for challenges, have processes that help them manage change and challenge, and time for team reflection on the challenges to allow team learning and growth after difficult periods.

I think it is really useful for leaders who want to manage the well-being and resilience of their teams to appreciate the two continua model of mental health (Westerhof and Keyes, 2010). The model proposes that mental health is *not* the opposite of mental illness. Mental illness and mental health are related but are *not* on the same continuum as seen in the diagram below; you can be mentally ill or mentally well, and on a separate continuum you can have poor mental health or good mental health.

Mental illnesses are diagnosed conditions that affect thoughts and behaviours. Mental health is emotional and psychological well-being. When someone has good mental health they can live a fulfilling life and are able to deal with everyday challenges. Mental illness such as depression and generalised anxiety disorder can mean someone languishes at work; however, they can also flourish. Their mental illness might be treated by medication and talking therapies – both prescribed outside of work – and resources to support their illness in work such as manageable hours, manager support and team relationships. Mental illness, just like physical illness or disability, does not have to prevent someone from flourishing.

'*Mental health is therefore best viewed as a complete state, ie, not merely the absence of mental illness but also the presence of mental health*' (Westerhof and Keyes, 2010).

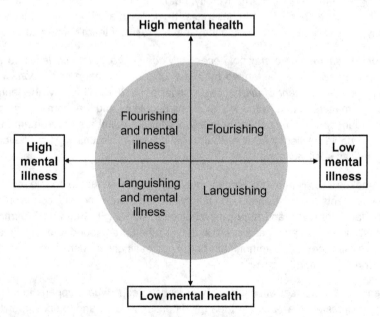

Figure 7.1 The two continua model of mental health adapted from Westerhof and Keyes, 2010

Developing resilient individuals and resilient teams is an ongoing process, not an end state. It's something that a leader can be continually mindful of managing, rather than seeing it as something to tick off the list, or complete. Developing resilience is a continual journey as life and work will always throw up new challenges, and there will always be change. Embracing the idea of it being a continual process of learning about resilience in yourself and others is a potently useful mindset. Resilience is not dichotomous, it exists on a continuum that is constantly changing.

PRACTICAL IDEAS TO INCREASE RESILIENCE

We will now look at some practical ideas that you can use in the workplace to develop resilience in yourself and others. Researchers have found in general that it is far better to focus on increasing protective factors (things that protect us from stress and adversity), rather than trying to reduce the risk factors that cause stress.

Managing your resilience level

One of my favourite writers on resilience is Chris Johnstone, who is an author and trainer who specialises in resilience and well-being. One of the tools that he speaks about is brilliant for using on your own or with teams in helping people to proactively manage their ability to be resilient. The tool is a perfect match for the ideas in positive psychology as it encourages people to look for the positive, look for strengths and be kind to themselves.

The exercise is called '*The Boat on the Water*'. Johnstone (2019) describes resilience as like rowing a boat over water. The water level is the resilience level. When the water level is high the boat moves along smoothly. When the water level is low the boat finds it more difficult; it is more likely to hit the rocks or be blown off course. There are things that happen or that you do that can cause the water level to go down. There are also things that you can do that increase the water level – your resilience level. You can brainstorm what pushes your water level down. Record these things on the left-hand side of the water level. These are the things that impact you in a negative way to decrease your resilience level. You brainstorm these to be aware of them, rather than to reduce them or prevent them – as often things that push our water level down are things outside of our control. You can then brainstorm: what pushes your water level up? These are things that you can do to increase your water level, your resilience level. On the right-hand side record what pushes your water level up. It is important that the things you identify that push the water level up are things that you can take accountability for and do. The exercise is so useful as when you start to recognise the triggers (the things that push your water level down), you are then able to proactively do some of the actions you have identified on the right-hand side to help increase the water level.

You can also do this activity as a team. I have run this exercise many times with teams to understand what things are pushing the team's water level down, and what would the team members like to do to increase their water level. This exercise helps in a number of ways. First, as people are encouraged to listen to each other about how they are feeling and what they are thinking, it helps team acceptance. It also helps enable agency in the team, as the team start to think about what *they* can do to increase their water level as a team, rather than saying we are having a hard time – what will others do about it?

The self-compassion break

This exercise can be used at any time of day and in any moment at work when you are feeling the pressure, or you want to help your team's resilience. Dr Kristen Neff is a pioneer in the study of self-compassion. She recommends the self-compassion break. This is about taking a moment in time when you are finding things difficult and harnessing kindness towards yourself to feel better and more able to seek the resources you need.

INDIVIDUAL PPI

Self-compassion break

- Stop and recognise that you are finding things difficult. Identify the negative emotion you feel and accept it without judgement. *This is accepting.*
- Recognise that life can be difficult, and others also suffer and can find life hard. *This is recognising common humanity.*
- Ask yourself: what can I say to myself to show myself kindness right now? *This is showing kindness to yourself.*

TEAM PPI

Team compassion break

- Stop as a team and recognise the team are finding things difficult, by letting the team share their current thoughts/feelings without judgement or defensiveness.
- Recognise as a team that working life can be difficult, and other teams and businesses face similar challenges.
- Ask the team: what can we do today to show kindness to ourselves and each other?

Recognise limiting thinking patterns

Our thinking patterns can greatly impact on how positive we feel. Performance-interfering thoughts (PITs) can impact our anxiety and stress levels and prevent us from being resilient at work. PITs are thoughts you have that hold you back, such as: '*I am not very good in these situations*'; '*I always mess events like these up*'; '*Everyone must know I am a fraud*'. When I use cognitive behavioural coaching techniques with my clients I often help them to identify their PITs so that we can work together to reduce them and increase their performance-enhancing thoughts (PETs). PETs are thoughts that encourage and enhance our performance.

The least optimistic people tend to have limiting thinking patterns that are based around the three Ps that were identified by Martin Seligman. These are: permanence, pervasiveness and personalisation. Negative events feel Permanent, they will last for a long time or forever; they affect everything (they are Pervasive); and the events feel directed at you Personally, or you feel that you are entirely accountable for what has gone wrong.

Alternatively, optimistic people tend to see negative events as:

- temporary;
- specific to a particular situation;
- not personal/external.

The first step in changing thinking patterns is to recognise them. Do any of these thinking patterns resonate with you?

- I just can't be like that.
- I am not as confident as other people.
- I am always stressed.
- I am an imposter – I am not really up to this.
- Others will think badly of me if I am wrong.

A way to manage PITs is to ask yourself questions like these.

- Does this thought really make sense?
- Is the thought helpful?
- What is a more helpful thought? This is a performance-enhancing thought.

Table 7.2 Performance-interfering thoughts vs performance-enhancing thoughts

Performance-interfering thought	Performance-enhancing thought
I just can't change	I can change, it will take time and effort, but it is possible
I am not as confident as other people	In time, I can be as confident as other people
Others will think badly of me if I am wrong	My view is important, and it does not matter if others think I am wrong; we can discuss it
I am always stressed	I can feel calmer in time

The thoughts we have about the past and the future can have a massive impact on the thoughts we have in the present. If your thoughts, or your team's thoughts, about the past are not enabling positivity in the present, then recognising the PITs that are leaving you or your team feeling hopeless or anxious or regretful and trying to identify the PETs is a way to enable resilience in individuals and teams.

While replacing PITS with PETs is a great way to enable resilience, for many people a crucial part of managing negative thoughts and emotions is acceptance, and this needs to come before replacing the PIT with a PET. This approach is a key idea in acceptance and commitment therapy (ACT). ACT is a type of therapy that encourages people to accept their thoughts and feelings without feeling guilt over how they think or feel. The therapy encourages people to accept what is going on in their head and their heart, as ACT is rooted in the belief that if you deny, ignore or fight against your thoughts and feelings they are immeasurably harder or impossible to change. ACT helps people to accept what they cannot control, and to identify and do actions that are within their control, that move them towards their desired future.

When difficult events occur we can sometimes find it difficult to accept the situation, we may fight against or deny the situation in our thoughts, or in the things we do, or distract ourselves with other thoughts so that we do not have to accept. Acceptance can seem like weakness, and if we accept that we feel embarrassed, or weak, or out of our depth, then we will be embarrassed, weak or incompetent. But accepting you are having a negative thought or feeling is not the same as accepting the content of the thought. For example, at work you may have the thought that you are incompetent because your team are not performing as you would like them to. You can accept and acknowledge that that is how you feel about yourself but realise that it is only a thought. The key to acceptance is being curious about the thought or feeling, interested in it but detached from it. While you believe the thought is a part of you, you become that incompetent person in your mind, and this is self-jeopardising, as then you are less competent to do anything about your team's performance.

Acceptance is about being willing to have painful or unwanted thoughts and feelings about something, being willing to make space for those thoughts/feelings and being curious about them. Being able to be with and accept strong feelings like anger, fear or bitterness is an important life and work skill. Your thoughts generate feelings that impact on your behaviour. As you open up and make space for these thoughts and feelings, they will bother you less. Thinking about metaphors can support you in changing the relationship you have with your thoughts, so that you can see them, accept them and respect them, without dwelling on them. This helps to enable you to move on and allows you to defuse from your thoughts. Harris, a leading expert in ACT, uses a metaphor for acceptance of walking across the ice.

> *Suppose you are walking across ice. In order to safely take the next step you first need to find a firm foothold.... Acceptance is like finding that firm foothold. It's a realistic appraisal of where your feet are and what condition the ground is in. It doesn't mean that you like being in that spot, or that you intend to stay there. Once you have a firm foothold, you can take the next step more effectively.*

(Harris, 2008)

I have seen the relief my clients experience when they realise that they don't need to deny the negative thoughts they are having, they don't need to suppress them, avoid them or feel awful for having them. The relief at being able to accept negative thoughts is liberating. Once the negative thoughts and feelings have been accepted, and looked at, then defusion from the thoughts is possible. You can then also think about the performance-enhancing thoughts you would like to have. Defusion from thoughts is astoundingly powerful because of the realisation that *you* are not your negative thoughts. The thoughts can give you information, they can be held lightly, and they can be let go of, but they are not '*you*' (Harris, 2008).

The '*commitment*' part of ACT is about encouraging people to commit to actions that move them towards their desired goal. In the case of working with PITs, you want to accept the limiting thought pattern, as we discussed, change your relationship with it, by appreciating that it is just a thought and not a part of you (you are more than just your thoughts), and then identify actions to move forward, for example, deciding on a performance-enhancing thought that will help and support you instead of the PIT. If you are interested in reading more about ACT, I recommend that you visit www.actmindfully. com.au/about-act/ which is the website of Russ Harris, a world leading expert in ACT. He says:

> ACT gets its name because it teaches us how to reduce the impact and influence of painful thoughts and feelings (acceptance) while simultaneously taking action to build a life that's rich, full, and meaningful (commitment).

> (Harris, 2019)

Manage inner voices

Sometimes the negative thoughts we have are like voices in our heads. Do you ever hear a voice in your head commenting on what you are doing, criticising you, hurrying you up or asking you a question? It may say '*Come on*', '*Oh, dear*', '*I used to be able to do this*', '*What's wrong with me today?*'.

Who is that voice in your head, that can narrate your life, interfere at key moments, make you more nervous when you want to be calm, and tell you what to do?

Tim Gallwey, considered the godfather of coaching, described the critical voice in our heads as Self 1, the ego mind. Self 2 is the '*doer*', the body that responds to Self 1 and does the action.

Gallwey first wrote about the two selves in the context of learning to play tennis. His book on tennis, called *The Inner Game of Tennis* (Gallwey, 1975), was predicted to sell 20,000 copies and has sold over a million. It is estimated that half of those copies have been sold to non-tennis players. What Gallwey wrote about was incredibly profound and useful within and outside of tennis. His ideas on the two selves apply not just on the tennis court, but in any sport, and any situation where you are performing (such as work performance, how you perform as a parent, how you perform as a friend).

Gallwey introduces the idea of Self 1 – the inner voice, and Self 2 – the doer. Someone playing tennis may hear a voice in their head saying, '*You should have hit that one*', '*Come on, make this count*', '*Run forward now and try to smash it*'. This is Self 1's constant narrative, telling the player what to do. Self 1 tells Self 2 (the doer) to perform an action, and Self 2 does it. But Self 1 does not trust Self 2 very much, and wants to constantly interfere.

Gallwey explains that it is the relationships between Self 1 and Self 2 that matters in performance. He says: '*In other words, the key to better tennis – or better anything – lies in improving the relationship between the conscious teller, Self 1, and the unconscious automatic doer, Self 2*' (Gallway, 1975).

He explains that, by improving the relationships with Self 1, Self 2 can get on with the doing. This relationship is the '*inner game*' that we need to play to ensure the '*outer game*' is successful. The best performance from Self 2 in the moment is when Self 1 is completely silent and still.

You may have often heard people say, '*I was nervous at first, but then I "forgot myself"*'. What do we mean if we '*forget ourselves*'? We mean we can no longer hear Self 1 commenting, asking, narrating, interfering, unnerving and meddling. We are just '*doing*'. And when we just '*do*' that is when we can reach great levels of performance.

Self 1's comments will often stem from:

- lack of confidence;
- anxiety;
- fear;
- perfectionism;
- frustration;
- anger;
- impatience;
- low trust (in one's own abilities);
- issues with identity (this just isn't me).

Paradoxically, Self 1 can offer positive feedback, but this is not always helpful in performing for Self 2. By listening to positive comments, naturally you know that if something is good, then something else is bad. You also know that if something is good, then there is pressure to keep it '*good*'. The best way to describe this is in Gallwey's words. He tells of a tennis coaching session when he was throwing the ball to coachees who were hitting it back. After a while he commented how well all the coachees were doing – and said, '*all the balls are together in the corner and not one at the net*'. The coachee who then had to hit the ball following that comment felt added pressure to hit the ball over. She then appeared more nervous and failed to hit many over. The positive feedback had had a negative impact on future performance by providing interference. She was now thinking, '*I must hit the ball over, otherwise I will ruin our good performance so far*'.

Therefore, the timing of positive feedback is important. If you are in flow, or you see someone in flow, breaking that flow with any type of feedback may impact performance. Interjections from Self 1 can add up to interference that impacts performance. Gallwey introduces the idea of the equation:

Performance = Potential – Interference

Your potential is within Self 2, but Self 1 provides the interference that reduces your performance.

The knowledge and understanding of Self 1 and Self 2 can be used to understand, reflect on and quieten your own self-talk. The way to quieten Self 1 is based on putting your attention on your body, rather than your ego. And noticing what you notice, rather than judging positively or negatively what is going on.

When Self 1 is ready with comments, or already commenting (such as, you are having a one-to-one with a team member and it isn't going well, or you are thinking about the work you need to do or a situation you need to deal with), the voice in your head may be saying '*You never handle these situations well*'. Or you are giving a presentation, and the voice in your head is saying, '*I'm nervous, I'm not good at this, why would they want to listen to me?*'

- Step 1 is to ask yourself what you notice about yourself and around you in that moment (your reflections may be '*I'm flustered*'; '*I am not communicating what I mean very well*'; '*I feel stressed about that piece of work I need to deliver*'; '*My chest feels heavy*' etc).
- Step 2 is to ask yourself what else you notice. This may be noticing what is happening to your heart, to your hands, to your voice or to your feelings, or it may be something else about you now. Be aware of what you notice, without judging it. This is key to being in Self 2. Judgement only occurs in Self 1. You need to exhibit detached observations.
- Step 3 is to ask yourself '*What do I notice now?*'

It is likely that as you notice things around you, and within you, they will change. And if you do this sequence frequently when faced with something that usually sets off Self 1, then Self 1 will gradually fade in that situation.

These steps may sound too simple, and almost self-defeating. How does noticing what is happening help? Noticing is bringing your attention to what is happening in the room and to you. If your attention is on what is happening in the room, without judging what is happening, then you are fully aware. And awareness is a fundamental route to change.

You may continue with the meeting, or the presentation, or the one-to-one, or you may continue with your day-to-day work. You can follow steps 1–3 as many times as you need to. They mirror elements of mindfulness – being in the present moment and accepting the present moment as it is.

By asking yourself to notice what is happening, you are also keeping Self 1 busy. There are other ways to quieten Self 1 by keeping it busy. An effective tool to keep Self 1 busy is to ask it to focus its attention on something. One of the easiest and most flexible things to focus on is breathing. Self 1 can focus on ensuring you are taking even, deep breaths and be aware of your chest rising and falling. In tennis, Gallwey says the player can focus on the stitches of the ball, or the intended arc of the ball. By focusing on these, Self 1 is distracted and forgets to tell Self 2 to get the ball in. I have experienced this many times when running workshops. Sometimes I will use a ball to throw to each of the delegates in turn, in a random pattern to introduce themselves or give their input. The delegates nearly always catch the ball. Some delegates express surprise that they did, as they say they cannot usually catch well. They catch the ball because they are thinking about what they are going to say, not about the ball. The distraction of thinking about what they will say quietens Self 1 – who might usually be saying, '*Make sure you catch the ball. It will look silly if you don't, go on pay attention, must catch the ball'* (or something similar). Keeping Self 1 busy allows Self 2 to get on with the job.

SUMMARY CHECKLIST

- Resilience is a trait you can develop and is something you can actively do.
- Factors needed at work for resilient individuals: self-efficacy, positivity, sense of coherence, social support, leader-member exchange.
- All the actions you can do from each chapter on PERMA will help support resilience for individuals and teams.
- A team of resilient individuals does not necessarily mean the team is a resilient team.
- A resilient team has a strong team identity, shared mental models, cohesion and trust between team members and strong psychological safety.
- Resilience can be improved for teams and individuals by using the metaphor of resilience being the water level, and you can look to increase the water level to ensure the boat can sail forwards.
- Being compassionate to yourself and as a team supports resilience.
- Thinking patterns and self-talk can have an important impact on resilience.

REFLECTIONS

To write this chapter I did a lot of reflecting on my own resilience, how my clients talk about their resilience and how the businesses I work with manage the resilience of their teams. What is really apparent to me is that the stories we tell ourselves about the past and the future have a profound impact on our resilience. When I say stories, I mean the narratives we use to describe what has happened to us, and what we anticipate will happen to us in the future. Interpreting past difficult times as struggles that left you damaged and weak is very different from interpreting past difficult times as struggles that left you stronger and wiser. Similarly, worrying about the future is very different to feeling hopeful or optimistic about what could happen, or your ability to manage whatever life gives you, and what you seek for yourself in life and work.

In the workplace, stories are often mentioned when people are looking to present with impact – a story capturing the imagination of the audience far more than data, figures and facts. That is exactly why the stories we tell ourselves capture our own imagination so well. They feel real and they incite emotion. Knowing this means that if you choose to tell stories about yourself that inspire, motivate, give hope, give you a sense of accomplishment, give you a sense of being connected to others and a sense of meaning (all the elements of PERMA), then what a difference that would make to how you think about the past and how you anticipate the future. If you manage people, helping your team to have a positive story about their past and a positive vision for the future is such a formidable path to increasing the water level and maintaining the resilience of the team no matter what difficult events they have faced or may face again.

SELF-COACHING QUESTIONS

Work through GROW for this topic and do add more questions/reflections at each stage than are detailed here if you want to explore further.

Goal (to uncover what your aim is)

- What specifically would I like to improve with regards to:
  - my resilience?
  - my team's resilience?

Reality (to understand)

- What is going on for me at the moment that is impacting my resilience or the resilience of my team?
- How will I know my resilience level has increased?
- How will I know my team's resilience level has increased?

Options (to explore)

- What could I do to increase resilience at work for myself and for my team?
- Who, apart from myself, needs to make a change in my team?
- What have I done already about this?
- What is stopping me from doing more?

Will (to decide on action)

- What will I need to do now?
- What is the first step I will take and when?
- What deadlines will I set for myself?

REFERENCES

Alliger, G M, Cerasoli, C P, Tannenbaum, S I and Vessey, W B (2015) Team Resilience: How Teams Flourish Under Pressure. *Organizational Dynamics*, 44(3): 176–84. doi: 10.1016/j.orgdyn.2015.05.003.

Bakker, A B and Demerouti, E (2007) The Job Demands-Resources Model: State of the Art. *Journal of Managerial Psychology*, 22(3): 309–28. doi: 10.1108/02683940710733115.

CIPD (2021) Employee Resilience and Evidence Overview. [online] Available at: www.cipd.co.uk/Images/employee-resilience-discussion-report_tcm18-91717.pdf (accessed 8 March 2023).

CIPD (2022) Supporting Employee Resilience: Guide for Line Managers. [online] Available at: www.cipd.co.uk/knowledge/culture/well-being/supporting-employee-resilience-line-manager-guide#gref (accessed 8 March 2023).

Gallwey, T (1975) *The Inner Game of Tennis*. London: Jonathan Cape.

Harris, R (2008) *The Happiness Trap*. London: Robinson.

Harris, R (2019) *ACT Made Simple*. California: New Harbinger.

Hu, T, Zhang, D and Wang, J (2015) *A Meta-analysis of the Trait Resilience and Mental Health. Personality and Individual Differences*, 76: 18–27.

Johnstone, C (2019) *Seven Ways to Build Resilience*. London: Robinson.

Krush, M T, Agnihotri, R and Krishnakukar, S (2013) The Salesperson's Ability to Bounce Back: Examining the Moderating Role of Resiliency on Forms of Intra-role Job Conflict and Job Attitudes, Behaviours and Performance. *The Marketing Management Journal*, 23(1): 42–56.

Lee, J H, Nam, S K, Kim, A R, Kim, B, Lee, M Y and Lee, S M (2013) Resilience: A Meta Analytic Approach. *Journal of Counselling and Development*, 91(3): 269–79.

Luthans, S, Avolio, B J, Avey, J B and Norman, S M (2007) Positive Psychological Capital: Measurement and Relationship with Performance and Satisfaction. *Personnel Psychology*, 60: 541–72.

Sharma, S and Sharma, S K (2016) Team Resilience: Scale Development and Validation. *Vision*, 20(1): 37–53.

Ungar, M (2019a) Interview by Pogosyan, M. How to Build Resilience. *Psychology Today*. [online] Available at: www.psychologytoday.com/gb/blog/between-cultures/201908/how-build-resilience (accessed 8 March 2023).

Ungar, M (2019b) *Change Your World: The Science of Resilience and the True Path to Success*. Toronto: Sutherland House.

Westerhof, G J and Keyes, C L (2010) Mental Illness and Mental Health: The Two Continua Model Across the Lifespan. *Journal of Adult Development*, 17(2): 110–19. doi: 10.1007/s10804-009-9082-y.

8   Well-being in action and conclusions

Understanding and supporting well-being is increasingly envisioned as an interdisciplinary issue that should be addressed at multiple levels within a system, including individuals, organisations, communities, and nations.

(Butler and Kern, 2016)

In this final chapter I draw together the ideas from each element of PERMA and draw conclusions. I will also talk about some examples of businesses that are successful in managing the balance of performance and well-being, and include thoughts from people I have spoken to in business on their views on the link between the two and how they work together to help people thrive. In this chapter we will zoom out from the individual PERMA categories and reflect on how to link the ideas from each element of PERMA into a well-being strategy that drives organisational performance and a culture of well-being.

WELL-BEING IN ACTION: THE PERFORMANCE EDGE

Through my research for this book, I have spoken to a number of people in business and researched successful businesses which have effective well-being cultures and good performance, to help crystallise my views on what I think '*well-being at work*' should mean to enable performance – I include some of those insights here. A key theme from my research, conversations and coaching experience is that well-being in business should not be just about contentment and is not merely the absence of well-being issues. '*Contented staff*' as a well-being goal would imply an organisation aspires for their employees to be in the comfort zone. The comfort zone definition is: '*a situation where one feels safe or at ease and a settled method of working that requires little effort and yields only barely acceptable results*'. Clearly, this would not lead to a productive and successful business. As we have looked at each aspect of PERMA, a theme that runs through each element is that there is so much more to well-being than just '*feeling good*' or feeling contented.

- Increasing the P shows us that increasing *positive emotions* motivate and drive us to do more.
- The E shows us that we are *engaged* when we have an element of challenge to our work that helps us achieve flow and use our strengths to grow and learn.
- The R shows us that *relationships* matter, and they help increase motivation and innovation.

- The M shows us that *meaning* is so much more than feeling good in the present, it is about having a purpose that makes sense and fulfils our potential.
- And A shows us that a sense of *accomplishment* in achieving motivational goals is incredibly powerful in building self-efficacy and self-esteem.

The positive psychology definition of well-being does not describe staying in the comfort zone, but says that well-being is a combination of each element of PERMA, a combination of positive emotions, engagement, relationships, meaning and accomplishments. Adopting the positive psychology definition of well-being would be an excellent way for organisations to have a well-being strategy that leads to high performance.

A good example of a company that has built a culture that focuses on its people and their well-being and happiness to drive performance is Timpson. Timpson is a British multi-national retailer with more than 1,700 shops that offer shoe repairs and key cutting. Ten per cent of their workforce are ex-offenders. Their strategy is based on the simple concept of trust. The culture of trust means people feel more engaged in their work, they build good relationships with their customers and they have more meaning in their work as they are empowered to make their own decisions. We have discussed all of these through exploring each element of PERMA.

In an interview with James Timpson, Chief Executive of Timpson, he said: '*We've always recognised that people are very important and always will be, I suppose we are especially good at looking after them compared to other companies*' (Lawrence, 2015). He also says in an interview in 2020: '*Our whole business is based on a culture of trust and kindness. When we talk about trust we only have two rules, which are #1 you put the money in the till and #2 you look the part. Everything else is a guideline … and guidelines are there to be broken!*' (Goodall, 2020). People in the shops are empowered to make decisions. Timpson measure their staff's well-being using a Happy Index, which asks on a scale of 1–10 how happy employees are with their area team or head of department or boss. It also has a free space for comments as well, for employees to expand on their feedback, helping them to feel listened to and empowered.

He also describes how the employees are treated with kindness, as if they were family, but importantly, he also says the organisation is not too '*soft*' as ultimately it is a commercial business. This supports the idea of well-being needing to be about helping people to thrive, rather than just helping them to feel content or happy. They encourage their managers not to tell people what to do, but to support their teams, and to act if people are not performing.

Richer Sounds is another example of a company that has a focus on well-being and happiness in the workplace, balanced with a focus on performance. Julian Richer, the founder and Managing Director, has recently updated his book (*The Richer Way*) on his approach on how to get the best out of people (Richer, 2020). He talks about his experience of leading Richer Sounds and acting as a consultant to other large organisations. Richer says, '*Many of the companies I have worked for are among Britain's most successful and progressive, but I have not yet found a company where there is no room for improvement in morale and productivity*'.

Richer Sounds is known for having the highest sales per square foot of any retail outlet in the world, and turns over £200 million annually. Richer places emphasis on work needing to be fun, and only making rules if they are absolutely necessary. He also passionately believes in recognising his staff, rewarding them when they do a good job, building a culture of feedback, and always developing and growing his people. These are reflected so well in PERMA, as we have seen through this book – reward and recognition build a sense of achievement, meaning and positive emotions (P and M). Feedback helps with building relationships, and keeping people engaged (R and E). Developing people supports all the PERMA categories.

Phil Jordan, who recently retired from the role of Chief Information Officer for the supermarket Sainsbury's and who has 35 years of experience in executive and non-executive roles, talked to me and described his view that well-being should be more than just '*nice*'. He talks about the '*performance edge*', which is language Sainsbury's use to describe a thriving employee who has focus and challenge in their work. Jordan describes how the focus needs to be on the well-being of teams, and on performance to ensure the business is profitable and teams are productive. He says: '*Employee well-being has never been more important, just as performance edge has never been more important.*' So how does Sainsbury's balance the two? It structures well-being support through three pillars: physical, mental and financial well-being. They have regular well-being campaigns, and have worked with the Samaritans and other retailers on a guide, *Wellbeing in Retail*, that is designed to support retail workers in looking after their own mental health, and to show how to help others. Jordan suggests that to balance well-being and performance, you need quality, tailored well-being services that you can signpost employees to, and these must be in combination with effective performance management, talent management and effective absence management. If you have a focus on well-being alone, then complacency and mediocrity can grow, leading to lower productivity. Or a focus on performance alone means unsustainable energy or passion, and eventually lower productivity. Jordan says: '*The only recipe for success is great well-being and performance edge.*'

WELL-BEING: LINE MANAGERS AND TEAMS

In certain types of businesses, such as manufacturing or retail, the role and requirements of different teams are vastly different. This means that what works for one team to support well-being might not be possible for another. It can mean that there are different customs and behaviours in different pockets of the business, depending upon what each team does and how they do it. Obviously, retail assistants can't serve people from home – they need to be in person at work, while the technology team can work remotely or even overseas. This means it is not as simple as creating one well-being culture to enable performance, and there may be cultures within cultures. This demonstrates the importance of line management in the specific areas of the business, tailoring how to meet the well-being needs of their teams to their specific roles. Line managers can only do that by listening to their teams, making time for well-being conversations and understanding the needs of their staff. Line manager capability in enabling high well-being (and consequently high performance) is a key lever for positive and productive employees, and is now a key component of effective leadership.

I spoke to George Culmer, who is Chair of the insurance company Aviva plc and Senior Independent Director of Rolls-Royce Holdings plc. Throughout his career he has seen line managers as having a key role in managing the well-being of their teams. He points out that it does not matter how great the well-being provision is in the business if people who are struggling do not actually access that well-being support: it can be the best provision in the world, but it won't help that individual. He emphasises that line managers need to be able to listen to their teams. He says: '*Teams need managers that can listen and understand the state of mind of their team members means they can support them in accessing well-being help if they need it.*'

A survey for line managers on well-being carried out by Management Today and the Institution of Occupational Safety and Health (IOSH) concluded: '*The positive impact they [line managers] can have on the well-being of their direct reports is huge, therefore it is vital they receive the best possible support from their organisations to empower them to champion positive mental health within the workplace*' (IOSH, nd).

In 2020 the CIPD developed new materials to help line managers support the health, well-being and engagement of their teams in response to the pandemic (CIPD, 2020). Their research found five key behaviours that line managers can develop that help support the well-being of their teams. These are:

- being open, fair and consistent;
- handling conflict and people management issues;
- providing knowledge, clarity and guidance;
- building and sustaining relationships;
- supporting development.

The CIPD emphasise that the behaviour of the line manager and the culture that the line manager creates for their team has the most influence on how an employee experiences work, and consequently has the biggest impact on well-being and performance.

One of the behaviours of the line manager is '*building and sustaining relationships*' – which is about building strong teams. We looked at the importance of relationships in the R chapter and how relationships enable well-being and performance. The feeling of '*team*' cannot be underestimated. When I come across people who are unhappy in their role, it can often be due to the relationships with their line manager, but it can also be their relationships with other team members, or the lack of '*team*'.

Culmer strongly emphasises the importance of team members motivating each other to thrive to enable well-being and performance. For him, well-being and team spirit belong together. He says, '*If a team has a collective experience of pulling together this does drive happier teams, a better outcome and better performance. There is a positive buzz being with like-minded people who are aspiring to deliver a common goal*'. In the top performing workplaces for well-being for 2022 in the UK, 92 per cent said, '*We are all in this together*'. The organisations with lower well-being had only 75 per cent saying, '*We are all in this together*' (Great Place to Work, 2022). Organisations that are getting it right on well-being do have a sense of people coming together to achieve.

WELL-BEING: REMOTE AND HYBRID WORKING

Tina Chander, Partner at a leading Midlands-based law firm that specialises in acting for SMEs, explained to me that she sees the situation of balancing well-being and performance from both sides. She speaks to employees who are feeling overwhelmed and stressed and don't want to continue at work or in their role, and she speaks to employers who are just not getting the output they need from their employees. She has seen a shift since the pandemic with employees being bolder about asking for what they require for their well-being, especially those who are moving to new roles and can negotiate on their packages, and that employers are having to respond to keep and retain talent. Some employers are embracing the changes, and others are having to change so that they can attract staff, with flexible working, either remote or hybrid, being top of the list of employee requests. Chander says, '*This is leading to a mutual shift of employees asking, and employers delivering*'.

Chander does have some hesitation in the increase of remote and hybrid working, and she cautions that it can bring less community. The R (relationships) of PERMA is much more difficult to build when people aren't working frequently face-to-face. She says, '*My concern is that if balance isn't "a balance", if you allow too much flexibility then employees could become lonely*'. The casual chit-chat that you would have in the office is much harder to create on MS Teams, Zoom or other virtual platforms. You are much less likely to message someone to ask what they are having for lunch than you would be if you bumped into them at lunchtime in the office. But it is these casual conversations that help build a sense of belonging and community. Having a Teams call is just not so fluid, and you miss ad hoc conversations that build unity.

Someone I coached recently explained to me that during the pandemic she was desperate to get back into the office as she loves to work with people, have lunch with others and be in an environment where others are working around her. She was delighted when people could return, but found when she was in the office some days she was alone or with a much smaller number of people. Other team members were staying remote or were not coming in every day. With this in mind, she reflected that she might as well be at home herself if she could not find the office buzz in the workplace. This brings us back to line managers. As Chander cautions, with people being in the office less often, it is critical that line managers do ensure they check in with staff on their well-being. Issues can be easily hidden when people are only seen on Teams, or don't turn their cameras on in Teams calls.

If you would find it useful to see which companies have been voted best workplaces for well-being in 2022 and 2023, then take a look at www.greatplacetowork.co.uk/. Great Place to Work has awards and reports on best places to work in the UK, Europe and the world.

For greater understanding of the specific well-being offerings in companies in the UK in 2022 the CIPD report *Health and Wellbeing at Work 2022* is a great resource. The report includes what UK organisations have in place to support well-being and useful benchmarking data on areas including absence, and well-being benefits (CIPD, 2022).

DEVELOPING A WELL-BEING STRATEGY

We have looked at well-being in action examples, so now let's consider how to build a well-being strategy that could be tailored for individual areas of the business and that empowers line managers. Designing any strategy is about being able to make synergies and create advantage. A well-being strategy needs to be synergistic with the organisation (size, sector, culture, location, structure), and create advantage for the organisation (through advantage for the organisation's people). As the first step in deciding what your strategy should be is understanding '*what is*', measuring well-being in some way is important.

Investors in People recommend measuring different areas to understand where your priorities should lie for your well-being strategy (Investors in People, 2022).

Table 8.1 Well-being topics and methods to measure them

Well-being topics	Possible method to measure
Employee satisfaction	Employee survey
Employee retention	Data from employee turnover Information from exit interviews on reasons for leaving
Employee motivation	Employee survey Productivity Absenteeism Presenteeism
Satisfaction with managers	Team survey 360 feedback by managers
Work culture	Employee turnover Employee absence Disciplinaries Complaints about management Absenteeism Presenteeism

While there are increasingly more organisations with well-being strategies, a recent survey found that half of employers surveyed said limited availability of data was holding them back in their well-being plans: '*only half (53 per cent) of employers reported being confident they could interpret and understand the impact of their wellbeing data on the organisation's wider business strategy, and only 10 per cent included this data in their annual reports*' (Howlet, 2020). Therefore, considering what data you will capture to measure your baseline and progress is crucial, and the targets that are set from that data need to align with the organisation's overall strategy.

The PERMA profiler

There are some useful well-being questionnaires that come from the positive psychology field. The PERMA profiler (Butler and Kern, 2016) is the first validated tool to specifically measure the five elements of PERMA. The profiler is a 23-item questionnaire that includes questions such as: '*In general, how often do you feel joyful?*' (measuring positive emotion). And questions such as: '*In general, how often do you feel anxious?*' (measuring negative emotion). The person must respond with an anchor from 0–10. For these questions the response anchor is 0 = never, 10 = always. This tool can be accessed online for personal use after completing a well-being measures registration form; and for commercial use this needs to be requested by contacting the Centre for Technology Transfer of the University of Pennsylvania. The advantage of this profiler is that it is based on a multi-dimensional view of well-being, which we have explored in this book, and it gives a result that shows the score for the individual aspects of PERMA, so you can see the elements of well-being in which you are thriving, and in which elements you can improve, which is useful and practical.

The profiler has been adapted for a workplace context, which makes it an incredibly useful tool for developing and measuring a workplace well-being strategy. The workplace version includes questions such as: '*At work, how often do you lose track of time while doing something you enjoy?*' The response anchor being from 0 = never to 10 = always. And '*Taking all things together, how happy would you say you are with your work?*' and '*How satisfied are you with your professional relationships?*'. The response anchor being 0 = not at all and 10 = completely for these questions (Kern, 2014). I completed the workplace profiler for myself for research for this book, and I found I really value the breakdown of scores for each PERMA category to see where I could improve to increase my overall well-being, and also where I am doing OK.

If you are interested in measuring your well-being at work and other specific components of positive psychology such as grit (perseverance), happiness, optimism and gratitude, the website Authentic Happiness has all of these for free to complete if you register (www.authentichappiness.sas.upenn.edu/testcenter).

If you want to design your own well-being questionnaire tailored to your organisation to baseline and track the success of your well-being strategy, consider:

- *keeping the questions simple, not including too much content other than the questions;*
- *not including lists of what has been done already on well-being;*
- *including at least one open-ended question for people to include some qualitative feedback;*
- *having questions on a five-point scale with a strongly agree to strongly disagree scale, which keeps it clear and consistent.*

(People Pulse Employee Engagement, nd)

Once you have baseline measures and decided on what your vison is for well-being in your organisation or team, the next step is to decide on your objectives for well-being. What do you want to achieve? It is crucial that the objectives fit with the overall organisational strategy and that if you have key measures of well-being that you have levers for improving and maintaining those measures (otherwise why are you measuring them?). For example, if you measure appreciation – what are you doing to ensure positive feedback (as well as developmental feedback) is given? If you measure loneliness, then what are you doing to build community and team relationships? If you measure absence, how are you ensuring it is not leading to presenteeism? If you measure output, how are you ensuring employees are not just working longer hours? How can you ensure you measure productivity, not just outcomes? Executing a well-being strategy successfully is the same as executing any strategy, gaining buy-in from key stakeholders, communicating effectively, involving the key people who need to help make change happen and reviewing results. If well-being is seen as a strategic priority to enable performance, rather than an end to itself, this ensures the well-being strategy has direction, focus and value.

CONCLUDING REFLECTIONS

In my coaching over the last 12 years, I have sometimes come across people who are finding work (and sometimes life) difficult. They feel overworked, disengaged from their purpose at work, and they are struggling to find the motivation to put in the effort that they previously found easy to do. Their reasons vary, but there are recent themes: the fallout from the pandemic; feeling isolated; lack of community in the office now that so many people are hybrid working; the number of unsettling events we have faced as a generation in the last few years (pandemic, Brexit, threat of recession, inflation); family pressures; and capacity issues. Whatever their reasons for currently feeling low and demotivated, ideas from positive psychology can help support people to increase their well-being, which helps their performance. I have used many of the ideas in this book in my coaching, and also apply the ideas to my own life and work. Ultimately, PERMA gives you agency – the knowledge that you if you do something in one of the areas, you can enable better well-being and then you feel well and can do more.

Reflecting on the five areas of PERMA and the R of resilience, we can see that to enable high well-being and ultimately performance, it is so much more than offering a menu of well-being offerings such as 'well-being' days to staff or gym membership. The Great Place to Work UK 2022 Report states that: 'An authentic culture of wellbeing is more than the sum of well-being-related programmes, perks and practices – although these can be hugely valuable if built on a strong and authentic foundation. This must be driven by a robust and holistic model of what drives well-being in the workplace and is regarded an absolute strategic priority driven from the top' (Great Place to Work, 2022). The emphasis here is on a strategic joined-up approach to well-being.

If we go back to my proposed definition of well-being at work in the introduction – to be bold and use ideas from positive psychology, seeing 'well' people as flourishing or thriving people – then the view of how to enable this needs to evolve. Well-being needs to encompass:

- feeling positive day-to-day (not just on the wellness day or on annual leave days);
- feeling engaged in the work;
- prioritising building relationships (and not just relationships to get the job done);
- finding meaning in work from the past and current work and meaning in the future;
- helping people to feel like they have accomplished something.

Well-being at work is about the culture or sub-cultures created across organisations through the behaviours people show day in and day out. Culture is not something that can be dreamt up in a boardroom, then disseminated on email. Culture lives and breathes in the thoughts, feelings and behaviours of the people in the business and that's why effective line management is so crucial. Line managers need to have the skills and confidence to listen to their teams, be aware of how they are managing their work and be able to signpost and motivate people to gain support when needed. This needs to happen whether people are in the office every day or they remote work. Effective conversations between people and their line managers can form the backbone of performance and well-being at work.

While I have spent time in this chapter talking about strategy and the line manager/leadership role in well-being, we must not forget that the responsibility for your own well-being also sits with you – leading yourself. Well-being strategies need to inspire people to want to look after their own well-being, seek the resources they need to manage/support well-being and encourage people to support the well-being of others. With this mindset organisations will have not just '*contented teams*', or the absence of mental health issues, but flourishing, thriving people and businesses. If you are looking to transform your performance at work using ideas from this book, a simple and powerful question is: '*What can I do to help myself?*'. Hopefully, this book is a great starting place for that with coaching questions, techniques and tips all rooted in positive psychology.

I'm conscious of the scientific research on endings from Daniel Kahneman, a Professor in Psychology. His research found that how something ends leaves a lasting impression on your memory of an event (or a book!). Therefore, I will leave the last word to Seligman as the founder of positive psychology and originator of PERMA, and a final question from me.

> *Habits of thinking need not be forever. One of the most significant findings in psychology in the last 20 years is that individuals choose the way they think.*

> (Seligman, 2011)

What habits of thinking will you take from this book to transform your performance at work?

REFERENCES

Butler, J and Kern, M L (2016) The PERMA-Profiler: A Brief Multidimensional Measure of Flourishing. *International Journal of Wellbeing*, 6(3): 1–48. doi: 10.5502/ijw.v6i3.1.

CIPD (2020) Support for Line Managers. [online] Available at: www.cipd.co.uk/knowledge/fundamentals/people/line-manager/introduction-to-support-materials (accessed 8 March 2023).

CIPD (2022) Health and Wellbeing at Work. [online] Available at: www.cipd.co.uk/Images/health-wellbeing-work-report-2022_tcm18-108440.pdf (accessed 8 March 2023).

Goodall, M (2020) Building Better Business: James Timpson Interview. Guild. [online] Available at: https://guild.co/blog/better-business-james-timpson-interview/ (accessed 8 March 2023).

Great Place to Work (2022) Wellbeing Now. [online] Available at: www.greatplacetowork.co.uk/resources/publications/ (accessed 8 March 2023).

Great Place to Work (2022) Wellbeing Now. [online] Available at: www.greatplacetowork.co.uk/assets/Affiliate-UnitedKingdom/Wellbeing-Now-report-2022-FINAL.pdf (accessed 8 March 2023).

Great Place to Work (2023) Wellbeing at Work Report 2023. [online] Available at: www.greatplacetowork. co.uk/awards/uks-best-workplaces-for-wellbeing-2023/ (accessed 31 March 2023).

Howlet, E (2020) Lack of Data Holding Wellbeing Strategies Back. People Management. [online] Available at:www.peoplemanagement.co.uk/article/1742884/lack-data-analytics-expertise-holding-wellbeing-strategies-back-survey (accessed 8 March 2023).

Investors in People (2022) How to Measure Wellbeing at Work. [online] Available at: www.investorsinpeople. com/knowledge/how-to-measure-wellbeing-at-work/ (accessed 8 March 2023).

IOSH (nd) White Paper Workplace Wellbeing. [online] Available at: https://iosh.com/health-and-safety-professionals/improve-your-knowledge/resources/workplace-wellbeing-white-paper/ (accessed 8 March 2023).

Kern, M L (2014) The Workplace PERMA Profiler. [online] Available at: www.peggykern.org/uploads/5/6/6/7/ 56678211/workplace_perma_profiler_102014.pdf (accessed 8 March 2023).

Lawrence, J (2015) Interview: John Timpson Chairman Timpson. HR Zone. [online] Available at: www.hrzone. com/lead/culture/interview-john-timpson-chairman-timpson (accessed 8 March 2023).

People Pulse Employee Engagement Surveys (nd) [online] Available at: https://peoplepulse.com/resources/ useful-articles/employee-engagement-surveys/ (accessed 8 March 2023).

Richer, J (2020) *The Richer Way.* London: Random House Business.

Seligman, M E P (2011) *Learned Optimism: How to Change Your Mind and Your Life.* London: Nicholas Brealey Publishing.

INDEX

Note: Page numbers in *italics* and **bold** denote figures and tables, respectively.

Printed in the United States
by Baker & Taylor Publisher Services